Praise for *Late Fascism*

'Toscano's wide-ranging, erudite study is both theoretically satisfying and politically inspiring – an essential reference for rethinking fascism and anti-fascist politics today'

—Michael Hardt, author of *The Subversive Seventies*

'*Late Fascism* is brilliant, incisive and right on time. We are living through a moment when the "F" word is no longer taboo, and the threat of fascism lurks everywhere. And yet, we are so mired in debates over definitions, typologies and analogies that our understanding of fascism remains elusive. Alberto Toscano avoids this trap by turning to *anti*-fascist thinkers, whose groundings in anti-colonial, anti-racist and anti-capitalist struggles remind us that liberalism is no enemy of fascism, and that fascists flower in the hot house of capitalism'

—Robin D. G. Kelley, author of *Freedom Dreams: The Black Radical Imagination*

'Alberto Toscano's *Late Fascism* brilliantly elucidates what Adorno once called "the meaning of working through the past" to grasp fascism's capacious aptitude for untimely reappearances to resolve crises, real or not, to save capitalism from itself and restore the necessary political order such rescue operations require. Rather than drawing upon fascism's past in his approach, Toscano's account persuasively lays to rest an interpretative scheme that explains such unscheduled repetitions by appealing to analogical comparisons of past and present as if they were the same. His own strategy positions history and memory against the present to disturb one another, unveiling uneven historical differences and incommensurables removed from an everyday dominated by exchange. Toscano's lasting achievement is the program of watchfulness he so carefully constructs to uncover the contemporaneity of late fascism in our midst, but never too late to recognize its ever-present morbidities'

—Harry Harootunian, Emeritus Professor of History, University of Chicago

'Can we speak of fascism before fascism? Alberto Toscano believes we can. In his learned excavation of debates across the twentieth century, he revives still unanswered questions about the location of the prison, the market and the bedroom in theories of fascism. He also reminds us to ask what late fascism is afraid of. What is it trying to prevent? In this way, a study of fascism becomes a roundabout recovery of repressed and forgotten utopias – a flashlight in the dead of night'

—Quinn Slobodian, author of *Globalists*

Late Fascism

*Race, Capitalism and
the Politics of Crisis*

Alberto Toscano

VERSO

London • New York

First published by Verso 2023
© Alberto Toscano 2023

All rights reserved

The moral rights of the author have been asserted

3 5 7 9 10 8 6 4 2

Verso
UK: 6 Meard Street, London W1F 0EG
US: 20 Jay Street, Suite 1010, Brooklyn, NY 11201
versobooks.com

Verso is the imprint of New Left Books

ISBN-13: 978-1-83976-020-4
ISBN-13: 978-1-83976-023-5 (US EBK)
ISBN-13: 978-1-83976-022-8 (UK EBK)

British Library Cataloguing in Publication Data
A catalogue record for this book is available from the British Library

Library of Congress Cataloging-in-Publication Data

Names: Toscano, Alberto, author.
Title: Late fascism : race, capitalism and the politics of crisis / Alberto
  Toscano.
Description: Brooklyn, NY : Verso, 2023. | Includes bibliographical
  references and index. | Summary: "Drawing especially on Black radical
  and anti-colonial theories of fascism, Toscano makes clear the limits of
  associating fascism primarily with the kind of political violence
  experienced by past European regimes"-- Provided by publisher.
Identifiers: LCCN 2023028670 (print) | LCCN 2023028671 (ebook) | ISBN
  9781839760204 (pbk) | ISBN 9781839760235 (US ebk)
Subjects: LCSH: Fascism--Europe. | Capitalism--Europe--History. |
  Racism--Economic aspects--Europe--History. | Crisis management in
  government--Europe.
Classification: LCC JC481 .T626 2023 (print) | LCC JC481 (ebook) | DDC
  320.53/3094--dc23/eng/20230728
LC record available at https://lccn.loc.gov/2023028670
LC ebook record available at https://lccn.loc.gov/2023028671

Typeset in Fournier by MJ & N Gavan, Truro, Cornwall
Printed and bound by CPI Group (UK) Ltd, Croydon CR0 4YY

For Brenna

y que se atreva el tiempo duro
a desafiar el infinito
de cuatro manos y cuatro ojos

And in memory of Lumi Videla (1948–74) and all those
who fought fascism in Chile fifty years ago

The problem of fascism is as old as capitalism. The threat was there from the start.

— Karl Polanyi, 'The Fascist Virus' (1934)

Fascism is a new name for that kind of terror the Negro has always faced in America.

— Langston Hughes, speech at the Third US
Congress Against War and Fascism (1936)

Contents

Preface

US President Joe Biden brands Republican backers of his predecessor as 'semi-fascists';[1] his Brazilian counterpart lambasts as 'vandals and fascists' the pro-Bolsonaro mobs who invaded the Congress in Brasilia on 8 January 2022; the mayor of Tel Aviv warns that Israel is sliding into a 'fascist theocracy';[2] Modi's Hindu-supremacist citizenship legislation is deemed the offspring of a 'fascist vision';[3] while Russia's invasion of Ukraine – grotesquely advertised as a 'denazification' programme – is seen to signal the regime's accelerating fascisation.[4]

Faced with the worldwide proliferation, consolidation and ascendancy of far-right political movements, regimes and mindsets, many leftists, liberals and even some conservatives have reached for the fascist label. The term is now bandied around with ease verging on abandon, particularly in the United States, but its resurfacing does speak to the urgent challenge of diagnosing the morbid symptoms that populate our present. This book is an attempt to contribute to a collective discussion about our reactionary political cycle. To write it, I turned to the archive composed by the theories of fascism produced in the past century, testing their capacity to shed light on our moment. What I found challenges many of the ruts, reflexes and commonplaces that debate on this extremely charged notion can and does devolve into.

This book is a record of my own path through materials from bygone conjunctures and disparate places, to salvage the components for a compass with which to orient myself. Are the novel faces of reaction usefully characterised as 'fascist'? Of the numerous and conflicting theories of fascism produced over the past century, which ones can provide some illumination in our dim times? What is the connection between the theorising or naming of fascism and anti-fascist strategies? My answers to these questions draw amply on the much-maligned 1970s debates on 'new fascisms', which I am convinced – polemical histrionics notwithstanding – remain more instructive for our moment than the deliberations of the Communist International, or, heaven forfend, Cold War disquisitions on totalitarianism. What I offer in these pages, then, is not so much a full-fledged theory, but a kind of metacommentary on fascism in our time, 'not a head-on, direct solution or resolution, but a commentary on the very conditions of existence of the problem itself' – one that must traverse a dense and fraught history of other, often militant, interpretations. Due to what Adorno diagnosed as fascism's 'intrinsically untheoretical nature', this approach is freighted with multiple challenges.[5]

The principal temptation for any contemporary thought on fascism is historical analogy. Faced with a toxic brew of social crisis, political violence and authoritarian ideology, the common sense reflex is to identify similarities between our present and the European catastrophe of the 1930s and 1940s, so as better to prevent its repetition (usually by reanimating liberalism as the sole antidote to illiberalism). Fascism is indeed a matter of returns and repetitions, but it is not best approached in terms of steps and checklists dictated by a selective reading of the Italian *ventennio* or the Third Reich.

Rather than treating fascism as a singular event or identifying it with a particular configuration of European parties, regimes and ideologies, for the purposes of thinking in and against our own day we need 'to see fascism within the totality of its "process"'.[6] This also entails approaching fascism in the *longue durée*, to perceive it as a dynamic that precedes its naming. It means understanding fascism as intimately linked to the prerequisites of capitalist domination – which, albeit mutable and sometimes contradictory, have a certain consistency at their core. W. E. B. Du Bois gave this core a name, still usable today: 'the counter-revolution of property'. For all their deep differences and dissimilarities, the Ku Klux Klan terrorism against Black Reconstruction, the rise of *squadrismo* against labour organising in Italy, or the murderous codification of neoliberalism in Chile's constitution can all be understood under that heading.

I do not intend 'late fascism' to operate like an academic brand, in competition with other names for our dire present. It is there to name a problem. At its most basic, like 'late capitalism' or 'late Marxism', it gestures toward the fact that fascism, like other political phenomena, varies according to its socioeconomic context. More provocatively, perhaps, it underscores how 'classical' fascist fixes – so intimately bound to the capitalist crises of their time, but also to an era of mass manual labour, universal male conscription for total warfare and racial imperialist projects – are 'out of time'. Ironically, many intellectuals and agitators leaning toward fascism today are actually profoundly invested in fantasies of a white, industrial, patriarchal modernity that have the *post*-fascist, post-war period as their seedbed. To recognise fascism's anachronism is cold comfort, especially when liberal and neoliberal fixes to planetary crises – especially to disastrous anthropogenic climate change – are themselves criminally late and inadequate, leaving much room for manoeuvre to the radical right, which is able to reinvent its fantasies of domination directed at 'women, nature and colonies' in profoundly destructive ways.[7]

An unreflexive struggle against fascism runs the risk of becoming sclerotic, self-indulgent or complicit with the very processes that body forth reaction, the lesser evil lending a hand to the greater one. When it does not question its own theoretical frameworks, its own habits of naming or indeed the pleasures of innocence, heroism and righteousness that may arise from these, anti-fascism can be its own lure.

I hope this book serves as an occasion to rediscover some pathbreaking anti-fascist thinkers, rooted in their turn in largely anonymous collective practices of worldmaking against domination, traditions of the oppressed which remain a resource for those set on dismantling the hierarchies that the partisans of Order and Tradition seek to revive and reimpose.

1
Out of Time

The spectre of analogy

Those who find themselves living in times of crisis and disorientation often seek shelter and guidance in analogies. The likeness of one conjuncture to another promises the preparedness necessary not to be found wanting *again*, to avert the culpable errors of precursors unarmed with foresight. A striking example, from Franco 'Bifo' Berardi, published two days after the election of Donald J. Trump as the forty-fifth US President:

> As they did in 1933, the workers have revenged against those who have long been duping them: the politicians of the 'democratic' reformist left ... This 'left' should be thrown in the dustbin: they have opened the way to Fascism by choosing to serve financial capitalism and by implementing neoliberal 'reforms' ... Because of their cynicism and their cowardice they have delivered people into the hands of the corporations and the governments of our lives. In so doing, they have opened the door to the fascism that is now spreading and to the global civil war that now seems unstoppable ... The white worker [*sic*] class, humiliated over the last thirty years, deceived by endless reformist promises, impoverished by financial aggression, has now elected the Ku Klux Klan to the White House.

As the left has taken away from the hands of the workers the democratic weapons of self-defence, here comes the racist version of the
class warfare.[1]

The analogy of fascism – itself inextricably entangled with its infra-
structural pair, the analogy of economic crisis – is both my starting
point and my critical target. My aim in this chapter is to reflect on
what some philosophically oriented theories of fascism formulated
in the twentieth century may indicate about the contemporary nexus
of politics and history, often by way of *dis*-analogies. I don't want
to rush an answer to the question, 'Is this fascism?' Instead, I want
to see what happens, what we can learn, when we project theories
of fascism onto the present.

To the extent that we can speak of fascism today, it is a fascism
largely emptied (albeit with important exceptions) of mass movement and utopia; a fascism shorn of what Ernst Bloch called
non-contemporaneity and Georges Bataille termed *hetereogeneity*; a
fascism that is not reacting to the imminent threat of revolutionary
politics, but which retains the racial fantasy of national rebirth and
the frantic circulation of a pseudo-class discourse. The latter is best
met not by abetting the sociologically spectral and suspect figure of
the 'forgotten' white working class, but by confronting what collective politics means today. Accepting this racialised simulacrum
of a proletariat is not a steppingstone towards class politics but
rather its obstacle, its malevolent and debilitating ersatz form. My
objective is to sketch out – for collective debate and dispute – the
elementary aspects of a pseudo-insurgency, with the caveat that a
pseudo-insurgency was in many ways what the murderous fascism
of Europe's interwar period also incarnated.

Most Marxist theorists at that time – for all their disputes over
the proper theoretical approach to the surge in violent reactionary
ultranationalism after the cataclysm of World War I – approached
the phenomenon of fascism at the interface of the political and the
economic. That is, they sought to adjudicate the *functionality* of the

fascist abrogation of liberal parliamentary democracy to the intensified reproduction of the conditions for capital accumulation, as well as its *instrumentality*, whether tactical or strategic, to particular fractions of the ruling class.[2] This meant defining fascism as an elite solution to the organic crisis of a profit regime confronted by the threat of organised class struggle amid the vacillations of an imperialist order. But it also meant recognising, at times, the contradictions between the possibility of a reproduction of the capitalist mode of production, on the one hand, and the autonomy or primacy of the political brutally asserted by fascist movements, on the other.[3] What was to be avoided was mistaking fascism's *exceptionality* – as an option undertaken in severe crisis conditions – for social and psychological *abnormality*. As Oliver Cromwell Cox provocatively observed shortly after the end of World War Two:

> The first error to guard against appears to be that of thinking of fascists and potential fascists as unsocial, degenerate people – gangsters; indeed, the very opposite of this is nearer the truth. Those persons in a capitalist society who finally organize in an active fascist party are mainly the most respectable and respected people … The fascists are the capitalists and their sympathizers who have achieved political-class consciousness.[4]

Without discounting the integration of sundry fractions of the US capitalist class with the Trump administration (from cement manufacturing to security, finance to private education, and above all fossil capital), and similar phenomena elsewhere (Brazil, India, Philippines and so on), the present conjuncture does not seem to warrant overly close analogies with that of the interwar period in terms of the dialectic of class and capital.[5] This is especially true in what concerns any organised challenge to capitalist hegemony – not least in light of ambient corporate protestations against state authoritarianism, the continued attraction of progressive neoliberalism for the maintenance of social peace and profitability, the risky prospects of protectionism and 'deglobalisation' and so on. Contemporary capital is ever happy to rely on state violence to shore up the prerogatives of private property, and keen to boost any political entrepreneurs aligned with its particular accumulation strategies. But – for the time being – it is not rushing en masse towards an exceptional state to counter existential threats to its reproduction.

Out of sync

The intensely superstructural, at times even fantastical, character of our present's fascistic traits would seem to warrant expanding one's focus beyond capital's strategies to shore up its social domination under conditions of crisis. In this chapter, I consider a number of theorists and arguments from the 1930s and beyond which, while accepting the formative nexus between fascism and capitalism, try to diagnose the ways in which fascist movements capture, divert and regiment surplus social energies – unrealised wishes for a better life, memories of precapitalist lifeways, unproductive and excessive desire. In so doing, I explore questions that will recur throughout the rest of the book: What is fascism's relationship to historical time? What is the place of classes, masses and groups in the imaginaries and strategies of fascism? Is fascism to be understood as a psychic and libidinal phenomenon, as well as a socio-political one?

One of the most heterodox entries in the interwar philosophical debate on fascism is Ernst Bloch's *Heritage of Our Times*. This protean, fascinating and unsettling work – which Walter Benjamin once polemically likened to spreading wonderfully brocaded Persian carpets on a field of ruins – contains a central, and justly famous, reflection on 'Non-Contemporaneity and the Obligation to its Dialectic'.[6] Like Georges Bataille, albeit in a very different register, Bloch approached fascism not as a political instrument or a psychic pathology but as a perverted utopian promise. Notwithstanding the important elements it neglected, this optic allowed the German philosopher to identify fascism's popular and energising features, which, in his view, its Marxist and communist adversaries had failed to effectively contend with and mobilise to their own ends.[7] Underlying Bloch's argument is the idea that society is criss-crossed by plural temporalities; the class structure of modern capitalism is shadowed by multiple cultural and historical times that do not exist synchronously. For Bloch, the Germany of the 1930s was a country inhabited not just by disenchanted citizens, restive workers and anxious exploiters. Crisis had pushed 'non-synchronous people' to the fore: declining denizens of pasts whose hopes remained unquenched, easily recruited into the ranks of reaction. The racist, conspiratorial occultism of the Nazis and their sympathisers tapped this lived experience of uneven development:

> The infringement of 'interest slavery' (*Zinsknechtschaft*) is believed in, as if this were the economy of 1500; superstructures that seemed long overturned right themselves again and stand still in today's world as whole medieval city scenes. Here is the Tavern of the Nordic Blood, there the castle of the Hitler duke, yonder the Church of the German Reich ... Peasants sometimes still believe in witches and exorcists, but not nearly as frequently and as strongly as a large class of urbanites believe in ghostly Jews and the new Baldur. The peasants sometimes still read the so-called Sixth and Seventh Books of Moses, a sensational tract about diseases of animals and the forces and secrets of nature; but half the middle class believes in the Elders of Zion, in Jewish snares and the omnipresence of Freemason symbols and in the galvanic powers of German blood and the German land.[8]

Where the class struggle between capitalist bourgeoisie and proletariat is a struggle over modernisation (the synchronous, the contemporary), many (perhaps most) Germans in the interwar period lived through social patterns and psychic fantasies embedded in historical rhythms other than the ones subsumed by the times of labour and capital. Mindful that it would be wrong to view any of these as merely primitive, in a country where social relations of production did not operate outside capitalism, Bloch wished to detect how, when it came to their fears (of social demotion or anomie) and desires (for order or well-being), these groups were somehow *out of sync* with the rationalising present of capitalism – the 'enlightened' space occupied by the mainstream socialist and labour movements and by their antagonists in big business. In a sense at once social and psychic, the political conjuncture was torn between the antagonistic and unfulfilled Now of capitalist conflict and the incomplete pasts teeming in its interstices. The collective emotional effect was a 'pent-up anger', which the Nazis and their capitalist boosters were able to mine and aggravate, while it remained off-limits to a communism whose rationalist principles risked generating irrational strategies. How were the organisers and intellectuals of the workers' move-ment to confront a situation in which a 'monopoly capitalist upper class … utilizes gothic dreams against proletarian realities'? Here the question of how to relate to the non-synchronous is pivotal, for it is useless to console oneself with the evolutionist just-so story according to which the archaic will gradually be eroded by social and economic progress. While the theory of the National Social-ists is not serious, Bloch writes, 'its energy is, the fanatic-religious impact, which does not just come from despair and ignorance, but rather from the uniquely stirring power of belief'.[9]

The political strategy of the proletariat must perforce be syn-chronous if it is to confront the capitalist Now – it must keep time with the rhythms of production and exploitation while being able to seize the time for strategically consequential action. But it is also called upon to recover and shape the kind of non-synchronicity from which spring immemorial and invariant demands of justice – the non-capitalist times of memory, fantasy or festivity that animate popular resistance. Bloch articulates this unfulfilled and 'unclaimed' task in terms of the relation between two forms of contradiction: on the one hand, the synchronous and determinate negativity of the organised proletariat; on the other, those 'subversively utopian' positivities that have 'never received fulfilment in any age'. The time of class struggle and material necessity had to make room for utopian time. Bloch was trying to supplement a thinking of the 'synchronous' contradiction between capital and labour with a sensitivity to the 'non-synchronous contradictions' that implicated classes out of step with the rhythms and sites of capital accumulation (peasants, petty bourgeoisie, aristocracy, lumpen proletariat, etc.), while also attending to something like a utopian unconscious in the proletariat itself.

As Anson Rabinbach notes, quoting from *Heritage*:

> The contradiction between these temporal dimensions demands what Bloch calls 'the obligation to its dialectic', a recognition of complexity which not only focuses on the synchronous, but on the non-synchronous, the multi-temporal and multi-layered contradictions within a single present. For Bloch it is precisely this sedimentation of social experience that creates the intense desire for a resurrection of the past among those groups most susceptible to fascist propaganda. For Marxism the problem is that fascist ideology is not simply an instrument of deception but 'a fragment of an old and romantic antagonism to capitalism, derived from deprivations in contemporary life, with a longing for a vague "other".'[10]

For Bloch, the point was to identify fascism as a 'swindle of fulfilment' – in his nonpareil phrase – while taking seriously the desires that fascism exploited. This meant exposing how fascism fraudulently reactivated unfulfilled pasts and unrealised futures. But is the complex dialectic of 'salvage' invoked by Bloch – for whom it is not just phases of emancipatory *élan* that could fuel revolutionary surges but also 'periods of decline when the multiplicity of contents are released in its disintegration' – a dialectic that could be reprised today?[11]

Doubt is cast on this possibility by all those perspectives which have emphasised, from the immediate post-war period onwards, the draining of cultural and temporal difference from the lived experience of advanced capitalist economies. A 'postmodern', 'one-dimensional' or 'administered' society is defined perhaps above all by this waning of historicity – which may of course be accompanied by the proliferation of history's instrumentalised simulacra. An interesting testament to this might be sought in the controversial newspaper articles of the mid-1970s in which the poet, filmmaker, and critic Pier Paolo Pasolini, shortly before his murder, sought to articulate the difference between an old and a new fascism. The latter – coterminous for Pasolini with a repressively hedonistic neo-capitalism and its mechanisms for securing total conformity – was marked by the obliteration of the past, in the form of what he called an 'anthropological genocide'. This hyperbolic formulation named the death of the experiences linked to peasant and 'popular' temporalities and forms of life, a genocide he would even register in the transformation of bodies, gestures and postures themselves.[12] For Pasolini, the old fascism of Mussolini and the Partito Nazionale Fascista was incapable of really undoing or transforming – we could also say 'synchronising' – those deeply embedded lifeways. This was evident in how pre-fascist plebeian forms of life had re-emerged seemingly unscathed after the downfall of the *Duce*. Contrariwise, the total power of contemporary capitalism to intensively shape and homogenise desires and everyday life, especially under the appearance of difference, choice and freedom, meant the destruction of all signs of historical unevenness along with all their utopian potentials. In the profoundly pessimistic view of Pasolini, and contra Bloch, there were no pasts left to salvage anymore.

How might we revisit this question of fascism and (non-)contemporaneity in our moment? Where do we stand vis-à-vis Bloch's explorations of non-contemporaneity and Pasolini's provocation, according to which the new fascism was based on the capitalist obliteration of any temporal and historical difference? We can begin by noting an enormous dialectical irony: the fascistic tendencies finding expression in the 2016 US election or in the contestation of its sequel, but also in coeval revanchist nationalist projects across the globe, are seemingly driven by a *nostalgia for synchronicity*, for the 'Fordist' heyday of Big Capital and Big Labour (generally coded as male and white) and for a certain ideology of modernisation. No archaic pasts or invented traditions here, but the hankering for the image of a moment, that of the post-war affluence of the *trente glorieuses*, for a racialised and gendered image of the socially recognised patriotic industrial worker (Bifo's national-workerism could also be termed a *national or racial Fordism*, which curiously represses the state regulation that its own fantasy presupposes). In this nostalgia for the contemporary, the industrial worker-citizen, the authorised emblem of a post-utopian depoliticised post-war modernity, now reappears – more in wish than in fact, no doubt, or in the galling mise en scène of coal workers flanking Trump as he abrogates environmental regulations – in the guise of the 'forgotten men', the 'non-synchronous people' of the political present. If this is a utopia, it is a utopia without transcendence, without any 'fanatic-religious' element, and with at best a feeble unconscious or unspoken surplus of popular energies.

Just as we must recalibrate Bloch's conception of fascist temporalities given the contemporary nostalgia for Fordist modernity (what we could term the non-synchronicity of the synchronous), so are we obliged to correct another heterodox theory of fascism, which also criticised the excessive rationalism of Marxist and communist anti-fascism – that of Georges Bataille. Bataille diagnosed the appeal of fascism's psychological structure, symbology and forms of ritualised organisation in terms of its manipulation of what he termed *heterogeneity*. With this notion, crucial to his philosophical anthropology of unproductive expenditure, Bataille named that which is incommensurable with the systematic self-reproduction of capitalist order, whether from below as mass excess, from above as unaccountable sovereignty or from beyond as sacred experience. As John Brenkman elucidates:

Heterogeneity, this affectivity and energy which concentrates itself in the subjectivity of the working class but is manifested throughout the population, Bataille argued, had been tapped by the fascist movement. Fascism in turn, however, tied this explosive affectivity back to the existing social relations by means of the set of symbolic forms, institutions, and political representations that were at once anti-bourgeois and anti-Marxist. Fascism found its support in the *force* of heterogeneity and its coherence in the fixing of this heterogeneity in authoritarian structures. In this way, fascism is the negation of its own affective sources.[13]

The fascistic tendencies of the present manifest a tenuous relation at best to such a system-wide libidinal surplus, except in the degraded, vestigial form of what we could call, by analogy with the psychoanalytic notion of the 'obscene father', the 'obscene leader' – or in the digitally mediated proliferation of masculinist groupuscules whose pagan posturing is saturated with the paraphernalia of neoliberal entrepreneurial culture and subjectivity, from bodybuilding to mail-order huckstering.

This too is linked to the absence of one of the key historical determinants of fascism, namely the revolutionary threat to capitalist order, which stood behind the demand that homogeneity inoculate itself with an 'imperative' excess (or its simulacrum) in order to survive. As Bataille noted in his 1934 essay on 'The Psychological Structure of Fascism':

As a rule, social homogeneity is a precarious form, at the mercy of violence and even of internal dissent. It forms spontaneously in the play of productive organization but must constantly be protected from the various unruly elements that do not benefit from production, or not enough to suit them, or simply, that cannot tolerate the checks that homogeneity imposes on unrest. In such conditions, the protection of homogeneity lies in its recourse to imperative elements which are capable of obliterating the various unruly forces or bringing them under the control of order.[14]

The limited significance of mass movements to contemporary fascist dynamics – which is only further underlined by the fact that today's racial-nationalist right advertises its movement character at every opportunity – could also be seen as testament to this deficit of heterogeneity and non-synchronicity, the feeble role or ultimate absence of the utopian and the anti-systemic, the sacred or the excessive, from today's germs of fascism.

Phony fanaticism, or mass psychology and its vicissitudes

To develop this intuition further, it is worth exploring in some detail the relevance of past debates about the mass psychology of fascism to our own moment. It was not only Bataille, in his writings of the 1930s, but many members of the Frankfurt School who saw Freud's 1922 essay 'Mass Psychology and the Analysis of the "I"' as a watershed in the study of the nexus between collective politics and individual desire, not least in Freud's analysis of the psychic life of leadership and followership. The influence of Freud's text was vast and variegated, but I want to consider it via a post-war text of Adorno's, 'Freudian Theory and the Pattern of Fascist Propaganda' (1951), which may also be taken as a kind of corrective to the salvage readings of fascism advanced by Bloch and Bataille.[15] The relevance of Adorno's text is only increased by the fact that it relates to research – namely his own participation in the collective project on *The Authoritarian Personality* and the book by Löwenthal and Guterman on American fascist agitators, *Prophets of Deceit* – which have been justly recovered to illuminate the Trump ascendancy and related phenomena.[16]

Löwenthal and Guterman ground their critical theory of the fascist agitator in the emotionally and intellectually paralyzing disorientation that marks social life subsumed by capitalism and beset by 'depersonalization and permanent insecurity'. They christen this condition as *malaise*, a kind of 'eternal adolescent uneasiness' to which the agitator 'gravitates … like a fly to dung'.[17] This malaise stems from a catastrophic impoverishment of the capacity for genuine experience, evidenced by the fact that 'people have learned to live in patterns' and tend 'to accept uncritically entire systems of opinions and attitudes, as if ideological tie-in sales were forced upon them', becoming 'stereotyped appendages of this or that big cultural or political monopoly'. Where fascism in power exploits at an industrial scale 'the connection between potential material poverty and real spiritual poverty', the agitators of *Prophets* do so in what we could view as a more artisanal, if no less sinister, fashion.[18]

What fascist agitation performs is a travesty of social change, 'something between a tragic recital and a clownish pantomime rather than a political speech'. The audience's malaise is reflected, teased, intensified, embellished and ultimately turned towards a scapegoat or enemy, in a 'call to the hunt'. And, while 'suffering from a kind of eternal restlessness, the agitator never seems to find a terminal and perfect image of the enemy'; in a 'striptease without end', the agitator and his audience find 'a temporary resting place' in their quest for a target in 'the Jew, who confirms the fantastic fusion of ruthlessness and helplessness'. What makes the agitator's vicious pantomime insidiously effective is the fact that he 'does not confront his audience from the outside; he seems rather like someone arising from its midst to express its innermost thoughts'.[19] Especially in its conspiratorial register, agitation gains much of its force from the fact that it does not propose any kind of theory but rather – in thrilling, salacious or sadistic detail – appears merely to mirror or corroborate the listener's own (worst) instincts.

As Löwenthal and Guterman astutely observe:

The agitator seems to continue the work of the muckrakers by courageously revealing why the powers that rule the world wish to remain hidden. But by dealing, as it were, with the audience's notions at face value, by exaggerating to the point of the fantastic its suspicions that it is the toy of anonymous forces, and by pointing to mysterious individuals rather than analyzing social forces, the agitator in effect cheats his audience of its curiosity. Instead of diagnosing an illness, he explains it as the result of an evil spirit's viciousness.[20]

This is just one of the ways in which agitation is, in Löwenthal's luminous phrase, a form of 'psychoanalysis in reverse'; in other words, the assemblage of 'more or less constantly manipulated devices to keep people in permanent psychic bondage, to increase and reinforce neurotic and even psychotic behavior culminating in perpetual dependency on a "leader" or on institutions or products'.[21] This link between the culture industry and fascist agitation constitutes more than a parallel or analogy, especially if we follow Adorno's observation that

> the mode of 'selling an idea' is not essentially different from the mode of selling a soap or soft drink. Sociopsychologically, the magical character of the word leader and therewith the *charisma* of the *Führer* is nothing but the spell of commercial slogans taken over by the agencies of immediate political power.[22]

Adorno too sought to theorise this protofascist and apparently anti-systemic, but ultimately conservative, intensification of malaise, which joins the feeling of agential impotence to the disorientation of the humiliated individual in the face of an enigmatic totality imagined as a limitless conspiracy. What he finds – especially since it relates to the forms of fascism in a post-war, that is, *post*-fascist, context – is more instructive for the present than the interwar philosophical reflection on fascism as a revolutionary phenomenon. Adorno wishes to move from the agitational devices singled out in *Prophets of Deceit* – which have as their 'indispensable ingredients ... constant reiteration and scarcity of ideas' – to the psychological structures underlying them.[23] As Peter Gordon has noted, Adorno's reflections are animated by his understanding of fascism as a phenomenon linked to the crisis of bourgeois individuality, understood as both psychic experience and social form.[24] Or, in Adorno's dialectical quip: '[We] may at least venture the hypothesis that the psychology of the contemporary anti-Semite in a way presupposes the end of psychology itself'.[25] As for Freud, Adorno observes that he 'developed within the monadological confines of the individual the traces of its profound crisis and willingness to yield unquestioningly to powerful outside, collective agencies'.[26]

Adorno homed in on the problem of the libidinal bond that fascism requires, both vertically towards the leader (especially in the guise of a play of narcissisms, the follower finding himself reflected in the leader's self-absorption) and horizontally, towards the racialised kin or comrade, identifying this as a key (psycho-)technical problem of fascist strategy. Commenting on the Nazi obsession with the adjective 'fanatical' and on Hitler's avoidance of the role of the loving father, Adorno remarks: 'It is one of the basic tenets of fascist leadership to keep primary libidinal energy on an unconscious level so as to divert its manifestations in a way suitable to political ends.'[27] This libidinal energy is of necessity personalised as an 'erotic tie' (in Freud's terms), and it operates through the psychoanalytic mechanism of identification (again, both horizontally and vertically).

At the psychoanalytic level, fascism preys on the contradiction between the self-preserving *conatus* of the ego and its constantly frustrated desires. This is a conflict that

> results in strong narcissistic impulses which can be absorbed and satisfied only through idealization as the partial transfer of the narcissistic libido to the object [i.e. the leader] ... By making the leader his ideal he loves himself, as it were, but gets rid of the stains of frustration and discontent which mar his picture of his own empirical self.[28]

What's more, 'in order to allow narcissistic identification, the leader has to appear himself as absolutely narcissistic ... the leader can be loved only if he himself does not love'.[29] Even in his use of language, the leader depends on his psychological resemblance to his followers, a resemblance revealed in the mode of disinhibition, and more specifically in 'uninhibited but largely associative speech'.[30] In sum, the

> narcissistic *gain* provided by fascist propaganda is obvious. It suggests continuously and sometimes in rather devious ways, that the follower, simply through belonging to the in-group, is better, higher and purer than those who are excluded. At the same time, any kind of critique or self-awareness is resented as a narcissistic loss and elicits rage.[31]

Yet the fact that the fascist leader often appears as a 'ham actor' and 'asocial psychopath' is a clue to the fact that rather than sovereign sublimity, he must channel some of his followers' feelings of inferiority; he has to be a 'great little man'. Adorno's comment is here instructive:

> Psychological ambivalence helps to work a social miracle. The leader image gratifies the follower's twofold wish to submit to authority and to be authority himself. This fits into a world in which irrational control is exercised though it has lost its inner conviction through universal enlightenment. The people who obey the dictators also sense that the latter are superfluous. They reconcile this contradiction through the assumption that they are themselves the ruthless oppressor.[32]

This loss of 'inner conviction' in authority is the salient insight of Adorno's reflections on fascist propaganda, and it is what allows him to move beyond the Freudian frame, still hamstrung by its reliance on the reactionary psychological energetics of Gustave Le Bon's 1895 *Psychology of the Crowd*. This relates once again to the hypothesis of the 'end of psychology', which is to say the crisis of a certain social form of individuality, which Adorno regards as the epochal anthropological context for fascism's emergence. The leader-agitator can exploit his own psychology to affect that of his followers ('to make rational use of his irrationality') because he too is a product of a mass culture that drains autonomy and spontaneity of their meaning. Contra Bataille's and Bloch's focus on fascism's distorting capture of revolutionary and utopian energies, for Adorno its psycho-social mechanism depends on a rejection of anything that would require the social or psychic transcendence of the *status quo*.

Fascism is here depicted as a kind of *conservative politics of antagonistic reproduction*: the reproduction of some against others, and, at the limit, a reproduction premised on the non-reproduction or elimination of the different, the other. Rather than an emancipatory concern with equality, fascism promotes a 'repressive egalitarianism', based on an identity of subjection and a fraternity of hatred: 'The undercurrent of malicious egalitarianism, of the brotherhood of all-encompassing humiliation, is a component of fascist propaganda and fascism itself' – it represents its 'unity trick'.[33] In a self-criticism of the psychological individualism that governed *The Authoritarian Personality*, Adorno argues that fascism does not have psychological causes but defines a 'psychological area', one that is shared with non-fascist phenomena and can be exploited and instrumentalised for state and capitalist interests in an 'appropriation of mass psychology'. In other words, fascism carries out 'the expropriation of the unconscious by social control instead of making the subjects conscious of their unconscious'. This is 'the turning point where psychology abdicates'. Why? Because what we are faced with is not a dialectic of expression or repression between individual and group, mass or class, but the 'postpsychological de-individualized atoms which form fascist collectivities'.[34] And while these collectivities may appear 'fanatical', their conviction is hollow, and all the more dangerous for that. Here lies the 'phoniness' of fascist fanaticism, which for Adorno was *already* at work in Nazism, notwithstanding its incessant broadcasting of the zeal with which it was carrying out the national and spiritual revolution:

The category of 'phoniness' applies to the leaders well as to the act of identification on the part of the masses and their supposed frenzy and hysteria. Just as little as people believe in the depth of their hearts that the Jews are the devil, do they completely believe in the leader. They do not really identify themselves with him but act this identification, perform their own enthusiasm, and thus participate in their leader's performance. It is through this performance that they strike a balance between their continuously mobilized instinctual urges and the historical stage of enlightenment they have reached, and which cannot be revoked arbitrarily. It is probably the suspicion of this fictitiousness of their own 'group psychology' which makes fascist crowds so merciless and unapproachable. If they would stop for a second, the whole performance would go to pieces, and they would be left to panic.[35]

This potentially murderous 'phony fanaticism' differs from that of the 'true believer' (recall the problems that revolutionary fascists, from National Bolsheviks to futurists, often posed to their own regimes); it alerts us to the role of performativity and bad faith in the spectacles of fictitious unanimity that are so essential to fascism's unity trick.

Jairus Banaji's reflections on contemporary fascism in India can complement this anatomy of fascist phoniness by foregrounding the place of violence within it. Banaji draws insightfully on Jean-Paul Sartre's reflections in his 1960 *Critique of Dialectical Reason* on 'manipulated seriality' – an atomised multiplicity at the mercy of external control. The fascist 'sovereign group' acts by transforming the serial existence of individuals in society – what Adorno had referred to as 'postpsychological deindividualised atoms' – into a false totality, be it that of nation, party or race (and often all three at once). 'Manipulated seriality is the heart of fascist politics,' as Banaji asserts, because it is not just *any* mass that fascism conjures up, but an *other-directed* mass that never 'fuses' into a group, a mass which must produce macro-effects at the bidding of the group 'other-directing' it, all the while remaining dispersed.[36] This is fascism's problem: how can the many act without gaining a collective agency, and above all without undoing the directing agency of the few (the group)? Banaji insightfully enlists Sartre's categorial apparatus to think through the fascist persecutions and pogroms that have punctuated Narendra Modi and the BJP's Hindu nationalist project ever since the Naroda Patiya massacre in 2002:

> The pogrom then is a special case of this 'systematic other-direction', one in which the group 'intends to act on the series so as to extract a total action from it in alterity itself'. The directing group is careful 'not to occasion what might be called organised action within inert gatherings'. *The real problem at this level is to extract organic actions from the masses' without disrupting their status as a dispersed molecular mass, as seriality.* So Sartre describes the pogrom as 'the passive activity of a directed seriality', an analysis where the term 'passive' only underscores the point that command responsibility is the crucial factor in mass communal violence, since the individuals involved in dispersive acts of violence are the inert instruments of a sovereign or directing group. Thus for Sartre the passive complicity that sustains the mass base of fascism is a serial complicity, a 'serial responsibility', as he calls it, and it makes no difference, in principle, whether the individuals of the series have engaged in atrocities as part of an orchestrated wave of pogroms or simply approved that violence 'in a serial dimension', as he puts it.[37]

That Sartre saw seriality as crucial to the very constitution of the modern state and its practices of sovereignty also suggests that the borders between fascist and non-fascist other-direction may be more porous than liberal common sense suggests. Yet we could also say that fascism excels in the systematic manipulation of the serialities generated by capitalist social life, moulding them into pseudo-unities and false totalities cemented by discourses of racial, ethnonational and religious supremacy.

Simulacra of class struggle

But how do phony fanaticism and serial complicity play out in the arena that would seem to define capitalist society as irredeemably divided and refractory to unification – class? If fascism operates through seriality, as a politics that is both other-directed and in which horizontal relations are ones of pseudo-collectivity and pseudo-unity – where I interiorise the command of the Other as my sameness with certain others – then we should be wary of analysing it with categories that *presume* the existence of actual totalities or even coherent groups. This is why it is incumbent on a critical (or indeed anti-fascist) left to stop indulging in the ambient rhetoric of the white working-class voter as the subject-supposed-to-have-voted for the fascist-populist option. This is not only because of the sociological dubiousness of the electoral argument, or the enormous pass it gives to the middle and upper classes, or because of the tawdry forms of self-satisfied condescension it allows a certain academic or journal-istic commentator or reader, or even the way it leads a certain left to indulge the fantasies 'if only we could mobilise them' and 'if only we had the right slogan'. Politically speaking, the working class as a collective body, rather than as a manipulated seriality, does not (*yet*) exist.

To impute the subjectivity of a historical agency to a false political totality is not only to unwittingly repeat the unity trick of fascistic propaganda but also to suppose that emancipatory political forms and energies lie *latent* in social life. By way of provocation, we could adapt Adorno's statement, quoted earlier, to read: 'We may at least venture the hypothesis that the class identity of the contemporary Trump voter in a way presupposes the end of class itself.' A sign of this is the stickiness of the racial qualifier *white* in white working class. Alain Badiou once noted about the phraseology of Islamic terrorism that when a predicate is attributed to a formal substance … it has no other consistency than that of giving an ostensible content to that form. In 'Islamic terrorism', the predicate 'Islamic' has no other function except that of supplying an apparent content to the word 'terrorism' which is itself devoid of all content (in this instance, political).[38]

Here whiteness is – not just at the level of discourse, but, I would argue, at the level of political experience – the supplement to a politically void or spectral notion of the working class; it is what allows a pseudo-collective agency to be imbued with a (toxic) psychosocial content. This is all the more patent if we note how, in both public debate and psephological 'expertise', whiteness seems to be indispensable in order to belong to this 'working class', while any determinate relation to the means of production is optional at best.

The racialised experience of class is not an autonomous factor in the emergence of fascistic tendencies within the capitalist state; it is the projection of that state, a *manipulated seriality*, and thus an experience different in kind from political class consciousness. In an incisive and still pertinent analysis, Étienne Balibar once defined racism as a supplement of nationalism:

Racism is not an 'expression' of nationalism, but a supplement of nationalism or more precisely a supplement internal to nationalism, always in excess of it, but always indispensable to its constitution and yet always still insufficient to achieve its project … As a supplement of particularity, racism first presents itself as a super-nationalism. Mere political nationalism is perceived as weak, as a conciliatory position in a universe of competition or pitiless warfare … Racism sees itself as an 'integral' nationalism, which only has meaning (and chances of success) if it is based on the integrity of the nation, integrity both towards the outside and on the inside.[39]

Many contemporary interpretations of national-populist 'revolts' against 'globalism' (like the pipedream of 'Lexit') risk turning class into a supplement of both racism and nationalism, stuck in the echo chambers of serialising propaganda. There is no path leading from the false totality of an other-directed racialised class to a renaissance of class politics, no way to turn electoral statistics and ill-designed investigations into the 'populist subject', the 'forgotten men and women', into starting points for rethinking a challenge to capital or for analysing and challenging the very foundations of fascist discourse. Any such practice will need to take its distance from the pseudo-class subject which has reared its head across the political scene.

This false rebirth of class discourse is itself part of the con, and another reminder that not the least of fascism's dangers are the fascination and confusion its boundless opportunism sows in the ranks of its opponents. Labour and production have returned as objects of nostalgic *ressentiment*: the superstructure as a dream of the base. Rather than thinking that a fully formed working class needs to be won away from the lures of fascism, we would do best to turn away from that false totality and rethink the composition of a class that could refuse to become the bearer of a racial predicate (white) or a national one (British). Class not as a carrier of the fascist virus, but its antibody.

The reactionary trope of the abandoned working class is a legacy of the capture, integration and promotion of class as a crucial operator in the workings of the twentieth-century national-social state, whose reality and representation continue to shape and constrain our present.[40] The post-war 'Fordist' compact cannot be understood without factoring in the nationalisation and racialisation of the working class, and without attending to the multiple borders that demarcated workers with social rights from the superfluous and the subordinate. It is not simply that, as Marx famously avowed, class was a product of bourgeois historiography and political economy.

A defence of the working class can very well be articulated in exclusionary and reactionary terms, which are not properly accounted for by the idea of a 'betrayal' of some naturally progressive impulse or of an unsullied history of emancipatory struggle – what Leo Löwenthal once called 'the myth of the spontaneous and creative forces of the exploited'.[41]

The contradictory, internally antagonistic history of the working class is not just a story of solidarity against the odds, or Sisyphean efforts to civilise capital and epic insurgencies to terminate it. It is also a record of 'hate strikes' for racially exclusive trade unions, passionate attachments to empire, chauvinism bolstered by ideologies of labour, anti-immigrant demands for a national preference in the labour market, fascism taking on the mantle of the 'proletarian nation'.

It is the latter anti-emancipatory history that we find indicted in Lenin's fulminations against social imperialism and the labour aristocracy, in Du Bois's enduring diagnosis of the psychological wages of whiteness, and in radical and Third World feminisms agitating for wages for housework and revealing the intimate bonds between patriarchy, racism and capital. Class is not just a name for social and political division; it must itself be divided, its historical fault lines traced, its ethical ruptures identified.

To cleave any conception of the proletariat away from the petty psychology of the masses is especially vital when our political imaginaries, across the spectrum, are saturated by strange replicas and refractions of a 'classical' class struggle that remains an object of nostalgic desire and misrecognition, a mirage of synchronicity in a time out of sync. Class politics as the practical negation of mass psychology: this horizon remains profoundly, painfully contemporary.

One precious clue for such a division can be drawn from a footnote to Walter Benjamin's inexhaustibly influential essay on the artwork in the age of its reproducibility. Chiming with, while innovating upon, the communist identification of the petty bourgeoisie as a key conduit for the politics of fascism, Benjamin operates a *détournement* of anti-socialist theories of the crowd to argue that it is not the proletariat, the lumpen or the poor who make up the modern crowd, but a fearful, reactive, compact grouping best captured in the figure of the petty bourgeoisie. As Benjamin observes:

> The mass [or crowd] as an impenetrable, compact entity, which Le Bon and others have made the subject of their 'mass psychology' is that of the petty bourgeoisie. The petty bourgeoisie is not a class; it is in fact only a mass. And the greater the pressure acting on it between the two antagonistic classes of the bourgeoisie and the proletariat, the more compact it becomes. In this mass, the emotional element described in mass psychology is indeed a determining factor ... Demonstrations by the compact mass thus always have a panicked quality – whether they give vent to war fever, hatred of Jews, or the instinct for self-preservation.[42]

In his perceptive essay 'Class', Andrea Cavalletti has glossed Benjamin in the following terms:

> When there is no solidarity or consciousness, there is no class; there is only the petty-bourgeois mass, with its well-behaved psychology ... The petty bourgeoisie is not, as Benjamin teaches us, a class: it is only a compressed mass between the rich bourgeoisie and the proletariat. From this non-class, every fascism will produce its 'people', masking this mere compression in the archaic and inseparable names of community, fatherland, work, blood, leader.[43]

In this perspective, the class difference between proletariat and petty bourgeoisie is a *political* difference, irreducible to stratification by income or differentiation by employment. Benjamin's suggestion that class consciousness should be understood in terms of a *loosening* rather than a becoming compact, and that class solidarity is pitted against identity and belonging, corroborates Adorno's words of praise in his otherwise sharply critical comments to his friend's work in progress on Baudelaire and the Paris arcades: 'Your few sentences about the disintegration of the proletariat as "masses" are among the profoundest and most powerful statements of political theory that I have encountered since I read [Lenin's] *State and Revolution*.'[44] Benjamin once famously spoke of making concepts 'unusable for the purposes of fascism'. Our current moment has made it urgent to carry out this operation for class too.

2
Racial Fascism

Swastikas bloomed in Chicago parks like misbegotten weeds.
— Martin Luther King, 'Drive to End Slums' (1967)

Nothing is more important than stopping fascism because fascism will stop us all.
— Fred Hampton (1969)

BALDWIN: It's very hard to recognize that the standards which have almost killed you are really mercantile standards. They're based on cotton; they're based on oil; they're based on peanuts; they're based on profits.
GIOVANNI: To this day.
BALDWIN: To this hour.
— James Baldwin and Nikki Giovanni, *A Dialogue* (1971)

Fascism was a monster born of capitalist parents. Fascism came as the end-product of centuries of capitalist bestiality, exploitation, domination and racism — mainly exercised outside of Europe. It is highly significant that many settlers and colonial officials displayed a leaning towards fascism.
— Walter Rodney, *How Europe Underdeveloped Africa* (1972)

Let us be reminded that before there is a final solution, there must
be a first solution, a second one, even a third.
                              — Toni Morrison, 'Racism and Fascism' (1995)[1]

It did happen here

Just as the aftermath of the 2016 presidential election witnessed the
mainstreaming of scholarly and activist discussions of fascism in the
United States and beyond, the frantic quickening of the news cycle
on the eve of the 2020 contest was again accompanied by multiple
efforts to check America's authoritarian pulse. Despite the deadly
farce of the January 6 white riot (America's own beer bong putsch),
the departure of the forty-fifth president made way for a rushed
remaindering in some quarters of the debate on native (or, better,
nativist) fascism. The Black radical perspectives on the fascist problematic surveyed in the following pages — with their commonly
neglected insistence on the structuring role of fascist potentials to
the US body politic — would suggest that we instead stay with the
trouble that briefly forced even some liberal partisans of American
exceptionalism to consider that fascism was not a dreadful anachronism imported from the Old World; that instead, to paraphrase H.
Rap Brown, it might be as American as cherry pie, deeply enmeshed
in histories of enslavement and extermination, dispossession and
domination that continue to shape the US present, materially and
ideologically.

While in 2016 attention gravitated towards the incoming administration's organic and ideological links with the extreme right
(Bannon, Miller, Spencer & Co.), the context of a mass civic insur-
gency against police murder and racial terror — the George Floyd
Rebellion — shifted the tenor and relevance of invocations of fascism
in ways that should be allowed to resonate irrespective of changed
occupancy in the Oval Office. In the months leading up to the 2020
election, the systemic challenge posed by mass Black-led movements against the racial and carceral state was displaced by the

US government onto the familiar figure of the (white) anarchist (or communist) agitator, as 'Antifa' became a target for William Barr's Department of Justice (still undecided whether this was a 'foreign terrorist organization' or an internal 'seditious' group). In the interim, the fauna of right-wing agitation grew weirder and more sinister still, thanks to QAnon, the Boogaloo movement, the Oath Keepers and the Proud Boys – who clearly took the presidential guidance to 'stand down and *stand by*' very literally. The state's exceptional powers – that dependable matrix of historical fascisms – were flexed in scenes of unidentified federal agents bundling protesters into unmarked rental vans and in the shooting of Michael Reinoehl by a US Marshals task force, even if further escalations did not eventuate.[2] Meanwhile, on the ideological stage, 'critical race theory' (along with the *New York Times*'s '1619 Project') was loudly proclaimed to be an 'ideological poison' that must be 'quickly extinguished'; the Executive Branch's Office of Management and Budget dispatched a memo to all federal agencies to 'cease and desist from using taxpayer dollars to fund ... divisive, un-American propaganda training sessions'; and an executive order condemned anti-racist critics for advancing a 'vision of America that is grounded in hierarchies based on collective social and political identities', a ludicrous case of projection if there ever was one. This very recent history should not be treated as a freakish blip; rather, as demonstrated by the persistence of the politics and personnel that made it possible (not least at the level of state legislatures that have ramped up their projects of racial disenfranchisement, dispossession and ecocide), it demands acknowledgment as the index of an entrenched and arguably burgeoning political potential.

Notwithstanding the changing terrain, talk of fascism has generally stuck to a familiar groove, namely asking whether present phenomena are analogous to those giving rise to interwar European fascisms.[3] Sceptics of comparison will underscore how the analogy of fascism either treats the present moment as exceptional, papering over US histories of authoritarianism, or, alternatively, is so broad as to fail to define what is unique about our current predicament. Analogy's advocates will instead point to the need to detect family resemblances with past despotisms before it is too late, often making their case by advancing some ideal-typical check list, whether in terms of the *elements* of or the *steps towards* fascism. But what if our talk of fascism were not dominated by the question of analogy?

Attending to the long history of Black radical thought about fascism and anti-fascist resistance – what Cedric Robinson called a 'Black construction of fascism', an alternative to 'the historical manufacture of fascism as a negation of Western *Geist*' – could serve to dislodge the debate about fascism from the deadlock of analogical thinking, providing the resources to confront our volatile interregnum.[4] Long before Nazi violence came to be conceived as beyond comparison, Black radical thinkers sought to expand the historical and political imagination of an anti-fascist left by detailing how what could be perceived from a European or white vantage point as a radically new form of ideology and violence was in effect continuous with the history of (settler-)colonial dispossession and racial slavery.

The pan-Africanist intellectual and activist George Padmore, breaking with the Communist International over its failure to think about the nexus between 'democratic' imperialism and fascism, would write in *How Britain Rules Africa* (1936) of settler-colonial racism as 'the breeding-ground for the type of fascist mentality which is being let loose in Europe today'. He would go on to see in South Africa 'the world's classic Fascist state' grounded in the 'unity of race as against class'.[5] Padmore's anatomy of what he termed 'colonial fascism' thus anticipated the memorable depiction of fascism as the boomerang effect of European imperialist violence in Césaire's *Discourse on Colonialism*. It was also echoed by the Tunisian-Jewish writer Albert Memmi, and by the Guyanese historian and revolutionary Walter Rodney, when he wrote of the 'fascist potential of colonialism' with specific reference to settler support for the Vichy regime and *pied-noir* efforts to destabilise liberal rule in metropolitan France.[6] The anti-colonial conviction whereby the standpoint of the targets of racial violence gives the lie to the exceptionality of intra-European fascism was also echoed by African American intellectuals. Speaking in Paris at the anti-fascist International Writer's Congress in 1937, the poet Langston Hughes would declare: 'In America, Negroes do not have to be told what fascism is in action. We know. Its theories of Nordic supremacy and economic suppression have long been realities to us.'[7] This was a lesson that could also be drawn from the monumental historical reckoning with US racial capitalism that is Du Bois's 1935 *Black Reconstruction*. As Amiri Baraka suggested, the overthrow of Reconstruction enacted a 'racial fascism' that long predated Hitlerism in its use of racial terror, co-optation of poor whites and passionate investments in white supremacy among ample sectors of the capitalist class, financial as well as industrial.[8] Reading the present via this lens can make palpable how and why 'institutionally the historical furniture filling America's political space has already been arranged in such a way that it would always leave open the prospect of evolving even greater authoritarian forms like fascism'.[9]

In this view, an American racial fascism could go unremarked because it operated on the other side of the colour line, just as colonial fascism took place at a spatial and epistemic remove from the imperial metropole. As Jean Genet observed on 1 May 1970 at a rally in New Haven for the liberation of Black Panther Party Chairman Bobby Seale: 'Another thing worries me: fascism. We often hear the Black Panther Party speak of fascism, and whites have difficulty accepting the word. That's because whites have to make a great effort of imagination to understand that blacks live under an oppressive fascist regime.'[10]

Fascism, prisons, and Black liberation

It was largely due to the Panthers, or at least in their orbit, that 'fascism' returned to the forefront of radical discourse and activism in the late 1960s and early 1970s – the United Front Against Fascism conference held in Oakland in 1969 brought together a wide swathe of the Old and New Lefts, as well as Asian-American, Chicano and Puerto Rican activists who had developed their own perspectives on American fascism (for instance, by foregrounding the experience of Japanese internment during World War II).[11] In a striking testament to the peculiarities and continuities of US anti-fascist traditions, among the chief planks of the conference was the notionally reformist demand for community or decentralised polic-ing – to remove racist white officers from Black neighbourhoods and exert local checks on law enforcement. It is not, however, to leading members of the Black Panther Party but to political prisoners close to the Panthers that we must turn for theories about the nature of late fascism in the United States. While debates about 'new fascisms' were polarising radical debate across Europe, the writing and cor-respondence of Angela Y. Davis and George Jackson outlined the possibility of theorising fascism from the direct experience of the violent nexus between the carceral state and racial capitalism.[12]

In one of his prison letters on fascism, collected in *Blood in My Eye*, George Jackson offered the following reflection:

> When I am being interviewed by a member of the old guard and point to the concrete and steel, the tiny electronic listening device concealed in the vent, the phalanx of goons peeping in at us, his barely functional plastic tape-recorder that cost him a week's labor, and point out that these are all manifestations of fascism, he will invariably attempt to refute me by defining fascism simply as an economic geo-political affair where only one party is allowed to exist aboveground and no opposition political activity is allowed.[13]

Following Jackson, we might ask: What happens to the turns and returns of the theoretical debate over fascism and (neo-)authoritari-anism when it undergoes a Gestalt shift and takes the racial capitalist state and its carceral apparatus as its fulcrum, in something like a '*tilt shot* angled from below' that might disclose 'a panorama of violence endured'?[14] As Jacques Derrida intimated in an unsent letter to Jean

Genet, dated one day prior to Jackson's assassination by a guard sniper at San Quentin:

> In a prison – this one and others – where it thought it had put its outside in chains, the system of (Western-white-capitalist-racist) society has made possible, by this act, the analysis of its functioning, a practical analysis that is at once the most implacable, the most desperate, but also the most affirmative.[15]

It has become commonplace in discussions of fascism to castigate the 1970s as a kind of cognitive nadir when fascism was degraded from a category of historical analysis and taxonomy into a one-size-fits-all political insult, with dire consequences. In what follows, I want to take the imprudent wager that there is virtue and insight in the seeming exaggeration or inflation of fascism in the context of seventies radicalism and liberation politics. But I especially want to underscore how viewing fascism through the prism of Black radical intellectual traditions can redirect our contemporary debate in fruitful and important ways. What might happen to our conceptions of fascism and authoritarianism if we took our bearings not from putative analogies with the European interwar scene, but, for instance, from the materiality of the prison-industrial complex, from the 'concrete and steel', from the devices and the personnel of surveillance and repression? Probing the analytical nexus of fascism and racial capitalism forged in the liberation struggles of the 1970s, we can also connect it back to the analysis of fascism emerging from Black theorists in the interwar period and forward to the afterlives of fascism in the late twentieth and early twenty-first centuries.

In their writing and correspondence, which is marked by differences of interpretation interwoven with a profound comradeship, both Angela Y. Davis and George Jackson identified the US state apparatus as the site for a re-emergence or indeed a perfecting of certain features of (European) historical fascisms. Much of their theorising is suffused by debates on the nature of monopoly capitalism, imperialism and capitalist crises, as well as, in Jackson's case, by an effort to revisit the classical historiography on fascism. Of note and relevance for contemporary concerns is the specific light that the prism of race – of racial domination and racial capitalism – sheds on the nexus of fascism and democracy, and how it can help us to interrogate and displace the normative conviction regarding the absolute antithesis between fascist despotism and liberal democracy. Jackson and Davis are profoundly aware of the disanalogies between present forms of domination and historical fascism, but they both assert the epistemologically privileged vantage point provided by the view *from within* a carceral-judicial system that could fairly be described as a racial state of terror. In distinct ways, they can be seen to relay and recode that foundational gesture of anti-racist and Black radical anti-fascism crystallised in Césaire's *Discourse on Colonialism*. As the Martinican poet and politician tells it: 'And then one fine day the bourgeoisie is awakened by a terrific boomerang effect: the gestapos are busy, the prisons fill up, the torturers standing around the racks invent, refine, discuss.'[16]

But the new form of American fascism that Jackson and Davis anatomise is not an unwanted return from the other space of colonial violence; it originates from the bosom of liberal democracy itself. The prisons are already full. And rather than a boomerang, the generalisation of racialised carceral terror into society at large – which is one of the foremost features of the new fascism – is a much less dramatic or sudden process of seepage, the permeation of the social space of actually existing liberalism by models and devices invented, refined and discussed amid concrete and steel. As Mullen and Vials justly observe:

> For people of color at various historical moments, the experience of racialization within a liberal democracy could have the valence of fascism. That is to say, while a fascist state and a white supremacist democracy have very different mechanisms of power, the experience of racialized rightlessness within a liberal democracy can make

the distinction between it and fascism murky at the level of lived experience. For those racially cast aside outside of liberal democracy's system of rights, the word 'fascism' does not always conjure up a distant and alien social order.[17]

Like Davis, Jackson also stresses the necessity to grasp fascism not as a static form but as a process, profoundly affected by its political and economic contexts and conjunctures. Whence the limits of models, analogies, or ideal types. Jackson comments on 'the defects of trying to analyse a movement outside of its process and its sequential relationships. You gain only a discolored glimpse of a dead past'; he remarks how, historically, fascism 'developed from nation to nation out of *differing* levels of traditionalist capitalism's dilapidation'.[18] Now, while for the author of *Soledad Brother* fascism is profoundly linked to a restructuring of the capitalist state, it is also fundamentally a counter-revolutionary form, manifesting in the violence with which it meets any substantive threat to the integrity of the state of capital. It is nevertheless instructive to note that, echoing Nicos Poulantzas's analysis in *Fascism and Dictatorship*, for Jackson fascism does not respond directly to an ascendant revolutionary force; it is a kind of delayed counter-revolution, parasitic on the weakness or defeat of the anti-capitalist left. The 'opposition of a weak socialist revolution' is thus a shared feature among the various fascisms (one can sense the indictment of the contemporary left in Jackson's historical allusion).[19] In a nutshell then: 'Fascism must be seen as an episodically logical stage in the socio-economic development of capitalism in a state of crisis. It is the result of a revolutionary thrust that was weak and miscarried – a consciousness that was compromised.'[20] Viewed from the US vantage point, that compromise is necessarily entangled with the persistent pattern of the racialisation of class that defines American history ever since the white-supremacist counter-revolution against Black Reconstruction, or indeed ever since Bacon's Rebellion and the concomitant 'invention of the white race'.[21] As Jackson quips: 'Marx's definition of history as a broken, twisted, sordid spectrum of class struggles is substantiated by Amerikan labor history.'[22]

Fascism in the United States had achieved a kind of perfected form for Jackson – all the more insidiously hegemonic because of the marriage of monopoly capital with the (racialised) trappings of liberal democracy. As he declared:

> Fascism has established itself in a most disguised and efficient manner in this country. It feels so secure that the leaders allow us the luxury of faint protest. Take protest too far, however, and they will show their other face. Doors will be kicked down in the night and machine-gun fire and buckshot will become the medium of exchange.[23]

Notwithstanding the national and conjunctural mutability of fascism, Jackson provocatively claimed that (economic) reform could be identified as 'a working definition of fascist motive forces', one that was particularly apt for the political expressions of US monopoly capital.

In Angela Y. Davis's concurrent analysis, the carceral, liberationist perspective on fascism is both further refined and shifted. For Davis, American fascism in the early 1970s took what was best described as a *preventive* and *incipient* form. The terminology was borrowed and adapted from her former teacher Herbert Marcuse. In a 1970 interview with Hans Magnus Enzensberger, Marcuse had proposed inverting the customary political sequence that would see fascism as reactive not just in social content but in temporal form – whether responding immediately to a potentially triumphant revolutionary upsurge or, in a mediated way, to an already defeated or ebbing challenge to capitalism. It is not reaction but anticipation that animates this new figure of fascism. As Marcuse tells Enzensberger:

I believe that there is something like preventative fascism. In the last ten to twenty years we've experienced a preventative counter-revolution to defend us against a feared revolution, which, however, has not taken place and doesn't stand on the agenda at the moment. In the same way preventative fascism comes about.[24]

The question of the possibility of fascism in the United States, much debated by liberation movements and the far left throughout the '70s and into the '80s, is for Marcuse deeply entangled with the concrete forms taken by 'preventative counterrevolution' as a core strategic imperative of the capitalist establishment, as well as its specific modalities of 'preventive counter-violence'.[25] The specificity of this anticipatory logic is also closely linked to the distinctive disanalogies between this 'incipient fascism' and its interwar European precursors. As Marcuse reflects:

The question is whether fascism is taking over in the United States. If by that we understand the gradual or rapid abolition of the remnants of the constitutional state, the organization of paramilitary troops such as the Minutemen, and granting the police extraordinary legal powers such as the notorious no-knock law which does away with the inviolability of the home; if one looks at the court decisions of recent years; if one knows that special troops – so-called counterinsurgency corps – are being trained in the United States for possible civil war; if one looks at the almost direct censorship of the press, television and radio: then, as far as I'm concerned, one can speak with complete justification of an incipient fascism ... American fascism will probably be the first which comes to power by democratic means and with democratic support.[26]

Fascism here defines a set of repressive tactics, as well as an encompassing political and ideological process, which differentially targets racialised and subaltern populations whose very existence and sociality are perceived as a threat – from the porous borders between the

'criminal' and the 'political prisoner'. It is a process in which – to
borrow from Jackson's characterisation of the 'oppressive contract'
underlying US capitalism – 'accrual of contempt [for the oppressed]
is [a] fundamental survival technique.'[27]

Davis develops the Marcusean thesis that 'fascism is the preventive counter-revolution to the socialist transformation of society',
specifying that transformation from the vantage point of the lived
experience of racialised communities in the United States.[28] For the
state, the most threatening feature of Black revolutionary politics
takes the form not so much of the armed struggle invoked by Jackson
but of the 'survival programs', the enclaves of autonomous social
reproduction practiced by the Black Panthers and other militant and
activist groups. What can be gleaned from Davis's account more
broadly are the differential visibility and experience of both fascism
and democracy. In this regard, it can help to attune us to the ways
in which race and gender, alongside class, can also determine the
modality in which fascism is lived.[29]

There is a kind of everyday fascism that marks the interaction of
people of colour with the state, and which, while acting as the repressive infrastructure of a liberal democracy still steeped in the legacies
of white supremacy, also signals the possibility or tendency to gen-
eralise incipient or preventive fascism to the population at large. As
Davis warns, fascism in the early 1970s is 'primarily restricted to the
use of the law-enforcement-judicial-penal apparatus to arrest the
overt and latent-revolutionary trends among nationally oppressed
people, tomorrow it may attack the working class en masse and eventually even moderate democrats'.[30] But the latter are, alas, unlikely
fully to perceive this phenomenon, both because of the making
invisible of its *site* – carceral space with its 'totalitarian aspirations'
– and the dilated character of its unfolding, of its time.[31] The kind of
fascism diagnosed by Davis is a 'protracted social process', whose
'growth and development are cancerous in nature'.[32] Davis's analyses
direct us to the prison as a racialised enclave or laboratory for the
fascistic strategies and tactics of counter-revolution, which are in

turn understood in terms of a molecular social process. Both spatially and temporally, the perception of fascist realities and potentialities is occluded by the opacity of their social and political infrastructure. As Davis would later write, in the context of her abolitionist activism:

> The dangerous and indeed fascistic trend toward progressively greater numbers of hidden, incarcerated human populations is itself rendered invisible. All that matters is the elimination of crime – and you get rid of crime by getting rid of people who, according to the prevailing racial common sense, are the most likely people to whom criminal acts will be attributed.[33]

Dylan Rodriguez has powerfully captured the originality and challenge of the 'fascism problematic' that Davis and Jackson forged out of the political violence of confinement. Notwithstanding their partially divergent evaluations, in naming a fascist present in the United States (whether incipient or accomplished), they share in 'a theoretical and symbolic political gesture that fosters an epistemological break from the common sense of U.S. white supremacy and the regime of state violence on which it is premised'.[34] This gesture is twofold. On the one hand, it anchors racial, carceral and counter-insurgent violence in political economy – not just by identifying the instrumentality of brutal repression to the reproduction of class relations, but by amplifying the Fanonian insight that we should consider violence 'as a *primary and productive* (rather than merely repressive) articulation of particular social formations'.[35] On the other, the reformulation of the fascist problematic from the vantage point of racialised political incarceration has the lasting virtue of troubling the facile if ideologically inescapable opposition of fascism and (liberal) democracy. As Rodriguez pointedly asks: 'How might our political understanding of the United States be altered or dismantled if we were to conceptualize fascism as the *restoration* of a liberal hegemony, a *way out* of crisis, rather than as the *symptom* of crisis or the *breakdown* of "democracy" and "civil society"?'[36]

As ever, rearticulating the analysis and aetiology of fascism also inflects the strategic imaginary of anti-fascism:

> The dynamic, strategic relations of violence condensing within the American social formation at different times and in different places are neither accidental nor excessive, and the challenge of this reconceptualized fascism problematic is to comprehend the socially reproductive capacities of coercive technologies and (proto)genocidal practice within the current order.[37]

From a complementary angle, Nikhil Pal Singh has illuminated the historical nexus between the 'preventive wars' waged by US imperialism and the fascist potentialities inherent to settler-colonialism and chattel slavery. As he writes:

> Poet Langston Hughes once described the casualties of U.S. expansion, slavery, and segregation as the victims of 'our native fascisms'; as careful scholars affirmed, fascism was largely a deviation of democratic regimes. Thus, while democratic liberalism continually reimagines fascism as its monstrous Other, fascism might be better understood as its doppelganger or double – an exclusionary will to power that has regularly re-emerged, manifesting itself in: (1) those zones of internal exclusion within liberal-democratic societies (plantations, reservations, ghettos, and prisons); and (2) those sites where liberalism's expansionist impulse and universalizing force has been able to evade its own 'constitutional restraints' (the frontier, the colony, the state of emergency, the occupation, and the counter-insurgency).[38]

As we will explore further in the next chapter, delving into racial and colonial fascisms – and into European 'historical fascism' as 'the last major drive for European colonial ventures in the twentieth century' – makes intelligible the superficially paradoxical notion of a 'fascist freedom' (and the subjectivities of the *Herrenvolk* liberals and democrats who promote it).[39] If fascism is also a product of the long history of 'race wars', then we cannot understand the fascist potentials of US nativism without attending, as Singh does, to the Indian Wars, and to the ways in which the settler-colonial organisation of dispossessive violence vested 'ordinary citizens with an expansive police power'.[40] Unlike classical European fascisms, US racial and settler-colonial fascism does not manifest univocally as the apotheosis of sovereignty, as a jackbooted Leviathan. Rather, as Singh observes:

> The construction of racist individualism and settler freedom that distinguished the Jacksonian democracy idealized by [Steve] Bannon, for instance, encouraged a slackness of centralized government control tethered to a violence exercised at its borders and margins, something that seemed chaotic, unstable, and disordered from the controlling seat of power. Considered in these terms, the Trump administration hardly needs organized paramilitaries to do its bidding, given the normative, historical, and institutional ways in which police powers in the United States operate as delegated and sovereign prerogatives to master and control indigenous and exogenous others.[41]

Arguments within Black Marxism

What relation might we trace between the fascism problematic differentially articulated by Jackson and Davis, on the one hand, and earlier theorisations of fascism by Black radical intellectuals, on the other? In a 1990 lecture that was published only recently, and which stemmed from an uncompleted book project on *The Black Response to Fascism*, Cedric Robinson advanced the proposition that chronic neglect of autonomous traditions of Black radical theorising has impeded engagement with that 'Black construction of fascism' that is alternative, indeed antithetical, to a 'euphonious recital of fascism' in mainstream theorisations.[42] Drawing on Hayden White's critical

anatomy of Western historiography, Robinson surveys the platitudes
and incoherencies of contemporary academic analyses of fascism to
reveal a founding conceit, an 'exemplary narrative' where the fascist
nemesis confirms the essential superiority of Western liberalism
and its Spirit, vouchsafing 'the existence of the epistemic West' and
the 'philosophic identity between Western civilization, Western
culture, and human destiny'.[43] Conversely, from the perspective of
non-Western peoples and Black radical movements, as Césaire had
crystallised in his *Discourse on Colonialism*, fascism

> was no more an historical aberration than colonialism, the slave
> trade, and slavery. Fascism was and is a modern social discipline [of
> domination] which much like its genetic predecessors, Christianity,
> imperialism, nationalism, sexism, and racism, provided the means
> for the ascent to and preservation of power for elitists.[44]

But, in keeping with the argument articulated in *Black Marxism*
regarding the autonomy of a Black radical tradition from Marxist
theory, Robinson is compelled to argue that most Black radical
theorists of fascism (including C. L. R. James, George Padmore
and Oliver Cromwell Cox) remained captive to the 'Euro-Marxist
construction of fascism', which subordinated the civilisational and
racialising continuities between Western colonialism and fascism to
economic determinism and class consciousness.[45] The signal excep-
tion to this, for Robinson, was Du Bois, who affirmed 'the cultural
identity between fascism and the putative democracies', anticipating
Césaire in arguing that 'the precondition for fascism was a civilization profoundly traumatized by slavery and racism.'[46]

There is something both intriguing and symptomatic in Robinson's conclusion that Du Bois's most forceful and resonant account
of the continuity between the history of white racism and fascism
'paradoxically ... coincided with that moment when Du Bois was
most influenced by Marxism'.[47] Was this really a paradox? Du Bois's
own account two decades earlier of the 'African roots' of World War I

had established a nexus between capitalist drives to empire and racist oppression that resonated with Lenin's contemporaneous treatment of imperialism; likewise, the pioneering account of autonomous Black agency (the 'general strike' of the enslaved) and insight into the capitalist infrastructure of racism in *Black Reconstruction* amply demonstrate that grasping the racial *and* capitalist origins of the West's disciplines of domination was an abiding concern for Du Bois.[48] To say that for Du Bois 'the essence of fascism was racial' is only persuasive as long it is not intended to refute the view that the essence of fascism was 'also' capitalist.[49] In other words, it is only if 'racial capitalism' is not reduced to a cultural or civilisational determinant of that massive if spectral discursive entity that is 'the West' that it can be articulated to the new phenomenologies of fascism that the likes of Jackson and Davis sought to explore – in ways that did not sunder insurgent Black movements from Marxist theories.[50]

The lived experience of state violence of Black political prisoners and its theorisation grounds a theory of US fascism and racial capitalism capable of interrupting narrow and clichéd images of fascism in mainstream political thought. It can still serve as an antidote to the lures and limits of the analogies that pervade and cloud mainstream debate. As the BLM movement has made patent, it is not the threat of a 'return of the 1930s' but the realities of racialised state terror that animate mass anti-fascist energies – which cannot be reduced to the necessary but insufficient task of confronting the ideologies and actions of more or less self-designated fascists. This does not mean flattening fascism onto the capitalist state and ignoring the autonomous threat that self-styled fascist and far-right movements pose in their mercurial shifts from system-loyalty to system-opposition and back.[51] But it is worth reflecting further on why theoretical perspectives on fascist potentials articulated by people of colour, drawing on lived experiences of racialised rightlessness, have often placed by far the greatest theoretical and strategic emphasis on organised state and capitalist violence rather than on the movements of the far right – sometimes leading to critical differences with an anti-fascist

left that saw those movements themselves as the primary reservoir
for the possibility of fascism (which is by no means to gainsay the
long history of militant self-defence of racialised and immigrant
communities against far-right non-state violence).[52]

The recovery of 1970s debates so often stigmatised for their exag-
gerations is not advanced here as an argument for a simple return
to the fascist problematic forged by Black political prisoners and
theorists. Notwithstanding the tenacious link between incarceration,
racism and capitalist power, historical disanalogies remain evident,
not least in the fact that contemporary authoritarianism is, alas, not
best approached in terms of its prevention of or reaction to revolutionary trends – though we may see it as a response to reformist
moves or to the threats posed to the racial order by urban riots and
insurrections. We might also benefit from recalling Stuart Hall's
warning, in the context of analysing Thatcherism and authoritarian
statism, about the dubious and self-defeating pleasures of a certain
anti-fascism:

> There is a sense in which the appearance of organized Fascism on
> the political stage seems to solve everything for the Left. It con-
> firms our best-worst suspicions, awakening familiar ghosts and
> spectres. Fascism and economic recession together seem to render
> transparent those connections which most of the time are opaque,
> hidden and displaced. Away with all those time-wasting theoreti-
> cal speculations! ... What we have to explain is a move toward
> 'authoritarian populism' – an exceptional form of the capitalist state
> – which, unlike classical fascism, has retained most (though not all)
> of the formal representative institutions in place, and which at the
> same time has been able to construct around itself an active popular
> consent.[53]

Visible fascists can distract us from more enduring and regressive
transformations, Hall suggests, while their absence can also serve
to minimise the profoundly violent and 'fascistic' mutations in the

state that may be invisible to the self-designated majority while being visited on the most vulnerable, as Davis intimates. But are we to remain stuck, when thinking our present, in an alternative between two positions, both seemingly compatible with the persistence of liberal-democratic institutions, however etiolated or distorted? On the one hand, *fascists without fascism* (the UK in the late 1970s according to Hall), on the other, *fascism without fascists* (which could be a way of defining the United States in the same decade, from the vantage point of its Black political prisoners). Perhaps, to bridge this antinomy we need to reflect on the connection between the kinds of 'incipient fascism' identified by Davis – in the US case, the intensification of forms of terror and pre-emptive repression against racialised and subaltern populations – and the emergence of explicitly fascistic movements and ideologies. In other words, we must attend to the mediations between the extreme levels of classed and racialised violence that accompany actually existing liberal democracies (think, for instance, of the administrative and military violence that pervades so-called 'migration crises') and the emergence of movements and ideologies which paradoxically argue that state and culture have been occupied by the left, that discrimination is now meted out against formerly dominant ethno-national majorities and that deracinated elites have conspired with the wretched of the earth and deviant others to destroy properly *national* populations that can be rescued only by a revanchist politics of security and protectionism.

Crisis and ideology

Our late fascism is an ideology of crisis and decline. In a powerful essay written in the wake of the 1992 Los Angeles uprising, Ruth Wilson Gilmore presciently bridged the Black radical theories of fascism forged amid the crushed revolutions of the 1960s and 1970s with the analysis of the mutations of racial capitalism in the age of so-called neoliberalism. Combining Robinson's internationalism with Jackson and Davis's insistence on analysing the nexus of state and capital, Gilmore argued that an analysis of the terror waged by the American crisis-state must be seen in terms of its articulation with a geo-economic order in which the United States was losing hegemony along with the capacity to carry out pacifying redistributions of imperial dividends. Continuing in the tradition of Du Bois's historical audit of the psychological wages of whiteness, Gilmore mediates the revanchist white supremacist ideologies crystallised around the trial of the LAPD officers who brutalised Rodney King and the concurrent impasse of US imperialism.[54] White nationalism here manifests as a crisis ideology, which is also to say a revanchist victimology, 'the idea and enactment of winning, of explicit domination set against the local reality of decreasing family wealth, fear of unemployment, threat of homelessness, and increased likelihood of early, painful death from capitalism's many toxicities'.[55] Racial ideologies do political-economic work, as civilisational narratives fuelled by ressentiment find outlets in policy platforms, exploiting 'the need for an enemy whose threat obliges endless budgetary consideration' – as writ large in the ensuing history of mass incarceration.[56] Psychic wages and racial dividends, steeped in the longue durée of *Herrenvolk* liberal democracy, shore up a brutally unequal regime of accumulation by enlisting bodies and psyches into endless culture wars that both prolong and obscure the ongoing social war within and the infinite wars without.[57]

At levels which are at once affective, ideological, political-economic, and planetary, incipient fascism returns here as the negative horizon of an anti-capitalist politics of liberation or abolition against racial capitalism and its authoritarian investments, catalysing the demand for combative counter-ideologies. As Gilmore noted, in terms that continue to resonate with the present:

> The very crisis which we must exploit – the raw materials of profound social change – is the tending toward fascism through the romance of identity, forged in the always already of the American national project. Our work is to rearticulate our own connections in

new (and frightening) forward-looking moves in order to describe,
promote, organize, bargain in the political arenas.[58]

As it has done so at repeated conjunctures in the US past
(Woodrow Wilson/the Klan/*Birth of a Nation* in the 1910s; George
Wallace/Richard Nixon/the 'Southern strategy'/'law and order'
in the late 1960s–early 1970s; Reagan and a far-right surge in the
early 1980s), the contemporary moment has witnessed the sinister
connubium between mainstream neo-authoritarianism, on the one
hand, and white nationalist or neo-fascist street and ideological
movements, on the other – with the latter often functioning as incu-
bator or intercessor for the former.[59]

In attending to the recombinant and plural character of contemporary authoritarian politics, it is worth reminding ourselves of some
methodological lessons from prior studies of fascism, racism and the
state. Especially pertinent to our moment is Poulantzas's warning
not to expect ideological cohesion or univocity from fascist ideologies. On the contrary, what the Greek Marxist theorist termed the
'popular impact' of fascism stemmed from its ability to modulate its
discourse in order to enlist and energise different class fractions, and
thus also to capture, divert and corrupt popular aspirations.[60] Or,
as the playwright David Edgar observed in his anatomy of British
fascism: 'The very contradictions of the doctrine, and their irrational
resolution, are at the core of its functional effectiveness as a mobiliser
of support.'[61] Now, whereas Poulantzas was analysing a historical
fascism deliberately playing across class registers, the contemporary
ecology of the authoritarian far right – including in the multiplicity
of its vectors of communication – can be seen to replicate fascism's
'pluralism' in a less centralised form, allowing tactical and strategic
convergences between authoritarian imaginaries that might seem
incompatible on paper. Approached from such a perspective, which
highlights the composite character of fascism as a crisis ideology
that accrues efficacy by dint of its contradictory character (not the
weakness a rationalist left may take it to be), the presence within

contemporary authoritarianism of neoliberal rationalities together
with (racialised) nostalgias for the 'working class' or aversions to
'globalism' is less of an enigma than it might otherwise be.

Poulantzas's insight into fascism's discursive pluralism can be critically enhanced by attending to Black radical perspectives on fascism
and authoritarianism, which force us to reintegrate what mainstream
critical theory often compartmentalises. Thus, for instance, to treat
racist authoritarian populisms as 'effects of neoliberal reason – its
expansion of the domain and claim of the private for persons and
corporations alike, and its rejection of political and social (as opposed
to market) justice' is to sever actually existing neoliberalism from its
imbrication with the changing imperatives of racial capitalism and
the reconfigurations of the racial state into an 'anti-state state'.[62] To
say that the 'energies of aggrieved power' that coalesce into contemporary neo-authoritarian and white nationalist ideologies 'remained
on the political fringe until recent years' – namely until 'a liberal
or social democratic order' was sapped by neoliberal reason – is to
imply a periodisation that would be largely unrecognisable to the
Black radical theorists and movements discussed above.[63] First – and
without discounting the way in which dimensions of liberalism or
social democracy were shaped by Black struggles, while also being
constituted by and constitutive of hierarchies of social difference –
racist ideologies and practices were never on the 'fringe'; witness
the fact that 'fascism' became an object of intense theorising and
disputation in radical Black (as well as Asian and Latinx) movements
in the United States during what is now retrospectively imagined as
liberalism's heyday. Second, the political emergence of neoliberalism as a discourse of state managers (rather than of an insurgent
intellectual elite) under Reagan and Thatcher was profoundly if
insidiously racialised from the start, and deeply shaped by the 'law
and order' agendas that developed in explicit antagonism to the
radical insurgencies of the late 1960s and early 1970s.[64]

The Black radical perspectives on authoritarian politics surveyed
in this chapter can contribute to overcoming the methodological

conceit that leads us to project typology onto history, treating 'liberalism', 'social democracy', 'neoliberalism' or indeed 'fascism' itself as political orders that can be exhaustively defined and recognised as operative in particular spaces and times. What if these defamiliarising perspectives force us to acknowledge that the political order is not 'one' – to recognise that, for instance, the United States has been '*experienced* as something uncannily similar [to fascism] by people of color living outside of its system of rights' at various junctures?[65] Fully assuming the differential, situated experience of authoritarian political orders and ideologies is the premise of a critical, reflective anti-authoritarian politics, one that confronts head on the material blockages to coalitional possibilities. Indeed, it was precisely this horizon of solidarities and their impasses that led the Black Panthers, Brown Berets and others in the late 1960s and early 1970s to turn to the discourse of anti-fascism.[66] This adjustment in our point of view also entails recalibrating our conception of fascism's history. Drawing on the rich archive of Black radical theories of fascism, we can start to see the present in a much longer historical arc, one marked by the periodic recurrence of racial fascism as the mode of reaction to any instance of what Du Bois once called 'abolition democracy', whether against the First Reconstruction, the Second Reconstruction, or what some have begun, hopefully, to identify as the Third.[67]

If one of the hallmarks of fascism as an inter-classist politics of domination – what I've termed its 'pluralism' – is the cynical amalgam of contradictory aspirations, a fatuous but fatal fusion of differences, then a creative appropriation of anti-fascist and anti-authoritarian traditions today will perforce require working through the fact that domination is not homogeneously experienced because it is not homogeneously exercised. It is on this background too that we may work politically to rearticulate our connections.

3

Fascist Freedom

The fascist love of freedom

While the practical work of halting and reversing the catastrophic march of the right is still lacking in strategy and force on too many fronts, the recent international debate on the new faces of reaction has been vibrant, if not always productive. In this chapter I address some of the problems that arise in revisiting the theoretical debate on fascism in an epoch whose governing ideology and dominant class strategy many still think are best captured by the idea of neo-liberalism – however mutant, recombinant or terminal the latter may be.

How, I want to ask, are we to conceptualise the connection between novel variants of what Karl Polanyi once termed 'the fascist virus' and the mutable instantiations of neoliberalism, beyond the familiar if fallacious assumption of a basic incompatibility between these two complexes of political ideas and practices?[1] Can a more nuanced theorisation of the place of the state in fascist and neoliberal practice provide some insight into the fascist potentials harboured by our current moment? And how might that theorisation relate to the vexed status of freedom in fascist discourse?

Received wisdom suggests that at the core of historical fascisms lay a violent aversion toward liberalism in all its guises, animated by an unchecked worship of the state as the hallowed vehicle for national and racial rebirth through inner- and outer-directed violence. Fascism, as the philosopher Giovanni Gentile – minister of education in the first two years of the regime and ghost-writer for Mussolini's 1932 'The Doctrine of Fascism' – affirmed, would thus be a 'statolatry'.[2] Conversely, the common sense about neoliberalism has portrayed it as driven by a veritable phobia of the state, a desire to limit the latter's interventionist hindrances to the freedoms of the market and the aspirations of the possessive individual or the entrepreneurial subject.

In the interminable seesaw of analogies and disanalogies that occupies so much of the public and academic debate about the contemporaneity of fascism, the notion of freedom has played a not insignificant, if at times muted or implicit, part. Liberal inventories of the elements of fascism will often identify the exaltation of the state and the repudiation of liberty as leading symptoms, finding contemporary movements and ideologies of the far right lacking in that department. Today's revamped authoritarian populisms spawn sundry Freedom Parties, and liberty is their leitmotiv – liberty *from* so-called 'medical totalitarianism', *for* and *of* property ownership, or as a marker of civilisational difference from migrants and their religions. There are choice examples of this trend in Andreas Malm and the Zetkin Collective's formidable panorama of an emergent 'fossil fascism':

> The doctrine of 'energy dominance' was annotated with some classical American freedom speak, when the Department of Energy in 2019 began to refer to fossil gas as 'freedom gas', to be exported without constraints around the world. Official documents from this Department, still headed by Rick Perry, spoke of fossil fuels as 'molecules of U.S. freedom'.[3]

Elsewhere, we come across Rainer Kraft, the climate spokesman for the xenophobic Alternativ für Deutschland, decrying the fact that mainstream parties in Germany are 'threatening the end of the world and stirring up mass hysteria, so that people will accept that more and more of their property and their freedom are stolen'.[4] But are the liberal, neoliberal and libertarian notes in the contemporary discourse of the far-right markers of an unbridgeable discontinuity with interwar historical fascisms?

I want briefly to explore the proposition that, in several ways, conceptions of freedom (at both the individual and collective levels) were not (and are not) alien to fascism, and that we may gain in our understanding of fascist potentials and subjectivities by tarrying with that apparent oxymoron, *fascist freedom*. As I will argue, this requires undoing our knee-jerk identification of fascism with a monolithic, bureaucratic state and its opposition to liberalism in all its forms. Fascism's relations with both liberalism and freedom are far more tortuous and less comforting than their assumed antithesis suggests. Undoing our common sense about the place of freedom and the state in fascist formations can also pave the way for a more nuanced understanding of fascist potentials within neoliberalism and how these might be seeded by racialised visions of capitalist order.

In his recent *White Freedom: The Racial History of an Idea*, the late historian Tyler Stovall, having traced the racial entanglements of ideologies of liberty across European imperialism, settler-colonialism and plantation slavery, judiciously observes that 'ideas of freedom did play a significant role in the ideology of fascism' – which should perhaps not come as a surprise given that those historical phenomena of domination shaped fascism's self-conception.[5] Writing in 1941 in the pages of *Studies in Philosophy and Social Science*, the English-language journal of the Institute for Social Research in exile, Herbert Marcuse would declare that 'under the terror that now threatens the world the ideal constricts itself to one single and at the same time common issue. Faced with Fascist barbarism, everyone knows what freedom means.'[6] Unfortunately, that may not always be the case.

The nightwatchman's bludgeon

Italian fascism's relation to liberalism was not unreservedly antagonistic. In the first years of Mussolini's regime, even a figure like Luigi Einaudi – later to become a member of the neoliberal Mont Pelerin Society and a president of Italy – welcomed the fascist government's efforts at balancing budgets and curbing social spending, describing them as a 'fruitful return of the Italian tax system to its classic liberal traditions'.[7] In 1923, Gentile, in the act of joining the Partito Nazionale Fascista, wrote to Mussolini himself:

> I have come to be persuaded that liberalism as I understand it and as understood by the men of the glorious right who led the Italy of the Risorgimento, the liberalism of freedom in the law and therefore in the strong state and in the state conceived as an ethical reality, is not today represented in Italy by liberals, who are more or less openly against you, but, precisely, by you.[8]

Mussolini himself would later declare: 'If liberty is to be the attribute of living men and not of abstract dummies invented by individualistic liberalism, then Fascism stands for liberty, and for the only liberty worth having, the liberty of the State and of the individual within the State.'[9]

Italian fascism's early identification with liberal conceptions of economic freedom is on display in the much-mythologised inception of its regime. On 29 October 1922, Mussolini was propelled to power by the March on Rome, inaugurating *l'era fascista*. In 1927, the regime would officially recognise it as the first day of Year 1 of the fascist calendar. Like any founding event, the March was also the staging of a spectacle and the forging of a legend. An early and opportunistic reader of Georges Sorel's *Reflections on Violence*, Mussolini was persuaded that politics was inseparable from mythmaking, that it was a kind of mythopoesis. In his Naples speech a few days before the March, he declared:

We have created our myth. Myth is a faith, a passion. It is not necessary that it be a reality. It is a reality to the extent that it is a goad, a
hope, faith, courage. Our myth is the Nation, our myth is the greatness of the Nation. And to this myth, to this greatness – which we
want to translate into a fulfilled reality – we subordinate everything
else. For the Nation is above all Spirit and not just territory.[10]

The myth of the Nation, of its lost and future greatness, continues
to animate the resurgent far right across the globe. Take the speech
delivered in October 2022 by the new Italian PM Giorgia Meloni,
prior to her successful vote of confidence in the Chamber of Deputies. Following a familiar script, invocations of national renewal were
accompanied by paeans to freedom advanced as antidotes to lingering
suspicions of authoritarianism. This is not freedom understood as
emancipation or liberation, but as market freedom yoked to what
Meloni, quoting Pope John Paul II, called the freedom of 'the right
to do what one must'. Without rushing to shaky analogies, revisiting fascism's origins can also serve to complicate its widespread
perception, defensively enlisted by Meloni, as liberalism's antithesis.

The March as myth – as the daring and virile show of strength that
spawned the fascist state – was not just hammered home in fascist
hagiography or in the retroactive *mise en scène* of the Exhibition of
the Fascist Revolution, first held in 1932. It also served as a model – a
consequential myth – for Mussolini's allies and admirers, above all for
the Nazis. Hitler's 1941 'table-talk' records the following assertion
about the 'heroic epic' of National Socialism's 'sister revolution':

The brown shirt would probably not have existed without the black
shirt. The march on Rome, in 1922, was one of the turning points of
history. The mere fact that anything of the sort could be attempted,
and could succeed, gave us an impetus … If Mussolini had been
outdistanced by Marxism, I don't know whether we could have
succeeded in holding out. At that period National Socialism was a
very fragile growth.[11]

So fragile, in fact, that when Hitler attempted his own putsch in 1923, it could be dismissed in the Italian press as a 'ridiculous caricature' of its fascist paragon.

In contrast to this mythology, historical accounts of the March tend to minimise its momentousness. Robert Paxton, in his lucid and synthetic *The Anatomy of Fascism*, attributes its success to the debilities and ineptitudes of the Italian political classes. It 'was not Fascism's force that decided the issue', he writes, 'but the conservatives' unwillingness to risk their force' against that of *Il Duce* and his men. 'The "March on Rome" was a gigantic bluff that worked, and still works in the general public's perception of Mussolini's "seizure of power".'[12] Salvatore Lupo, in his study of Italian fascism's political history, likewise notes that, with the March,

> the provincial Italy of *squadrismo* wished to force the hand of that vast swathe of the liberal-conservative [*liberal-moderato*], monarchist, military and capitalist [*confindustriale*] establishment which looked upon the Black Shirts with sympathy but which needed to feel some menacing pressure in order to abandon the option of a centre-right government.[13]

Seen in this light, the March on Rome was not a heroic epic, but the achievement of 'a maximum result with minimal risk', in Emilio Gentile's formulation.[14]

While it is useful to undermine fascism's self-regarding myths, we should be wary of magnifying its parasitism on the weakness of its enemies and the complicity of its beneficiaries. In so doing, we risk presenting it as an insubstantial, almost inexplicable phenomenon. Bending the stick somewhat in the other direction, it is instructive to turn to the treatment of the March by that inspired and ambiguous chronicler of his age, Curzio Malaparte. In his 1931 *Technique of the Coup d'État*, which Mussolini banned so as not to displease Hitler (who was roundly ridiculed in unflattering comparisons to the *Duce*), Malaparte, an early participant in *squadrismo* and a 'left' fascist, irreverently comments that Mussolini could only have commanded the 'fascist insurrectional machine' as he did because of his 'Marxism'. By this Malaparte perversely meant Mussolini's recognition of the strategic importance of defeating the working class — a victory that would also sap any force of resistance within the state.

What Malaparte ends up describing is something like a *tactics of the void*. As he observes:

> It was a matter not just of preventing the general strike, but also the united front of Government, Parliament and the proletariat. Fascism faced the necessity of making a void around itself, of making a *tabula rasa* of every organized force, whether political or syndicalist, proletarian or bourgeois, trade unions, cooperatives, workers' circles, Labour Exchanges (*Camere del lavoro*), newspapers, political parties.[15]

The fascist insurrectional machine was a formidable apparatus for the organisation of dis-organisation, the hyperpolitical imposition of a deadening depoliticisation — something that it carried out on the parallel tracks of direct violence and corridor conspiracies. Malaparte signals the logistical intelligence that went into the tactics of what *The Guardian* described at the time as a 'bloodless revolution'. Not so much the streets or the most visible centres of power, but various material and institutional nodes — key points in Italy's network of political energy — were the focus of the *squadristi* in the preparatory stages of the March. As Malaparte recounts:

> The black shirts had occupied by surprise all the strategic points of city and country, namely the organs of technical organization, gasworks, electricity plants, central post offices, telephone and telegraph exchanges, bridges, railway stations. The political and military authorities were caught unprepared by this sudden attack.[16]

Hence the melancholy insight in the avowal of Giovanni Giolitti, the long-serving prime minister of Italy during the first two decades of the twentieth century: 'I am indebted to Mussolini for having learned that it is not against the programme of a revolution that a state must defend itself, but against its tactics.'[17]

But what programme accompanied these tactics? This is where a simple antithesis between fascism and liberalism starts to unravel. The Gramsci scholar Fabio Frosini has recently compiled an excellent critical anthology of Mussolini's speeches and writings from 1921 to 1932 under the title *The Construction of the New State*. The pronouncements leading up to the March largely resonate with Malaparte's conception. *Squadrismo*'s violent methods were underpinned by a pseudo-Nietzschean aristocratism that contrasted the transformative power of warrior elites with the pacifist tendencies of the proletariat. In his inaugural speech at the Chamber of Deputies, Mussolini declaimed that

> it is beyond dispute, by now, that on the terrain of violence the working masses will be defeated ... the working masses are naturally, I would dare say blessedly, peace-mongering, because they always represent the static reserves of human societies, while risk, danger, the taste for adventure have always been the task and privilege of small aristocracies.[18]

This 'anthropological' dismissal of the masses' capacity for struggle was accompanied by a repudiation of Marxism, understood as an amalgam of state socialism and the theory of class struggle as historical motor: 'We deny that there exist two classes because there exist many more, we deny that the whole of human history can be explained by economic determinism.' In fascism's 'synthesis of the antitheses' – class *and* nation – internationalism was to be vigorously repelled. For Mussolini, in a formula that finds myriad echoes in the rhetoric of contemporary reaction, internationalism was a 'luxury commodity, which can only be practiced by the upper classes, while the people are desperately tied to their native land'.[19]

But fascism's *modus operandi* before the March on Rome was not just a war against class war. Jettisoning its prior republicanism for opportunistic encomia to army and king, it crystallised into a project of *public violence for private capital*. While the construction of the fascist state eventually entailed significant movement towards administrative centralisation and involvement in the economic sphere, the Mussolini of 1921–22 was emphatic about the fundamentally *liberal* economic philosophy of fascism. In his inaugural parliamentary speech, Mussolini told his left-wing opponents that revisionist socialist literature had imbued him with the conviction that 'only now is the true history of capitalism beginning, because capitalism is not only a system of oppression, but also a selection of values, a coordination of hierarchies, a more amply developed sense of individual responsibility'.[20]

A belief in capitalism's vitality supported the planned shrinkage of the state initially demanded by the fascist leader. Saving the state, he argued, called for a 'surgical operation'. If the state had one hundred arms, ninety-five required amputation, given 'the need to reduce the state to its purely juridical and political expression'. Reading passages like the following, it is hardly mysterious why the likes of Ludwig von Mises greeted fascism's surge as liberalism's salvation:

> Let the State give us a police force, to save gentlemen from scoundrels, an army ready for any eventuality, a foreign policy attuned to national necessities. Everything else, and I am not even excluding secondary education, belongs to the private activity of the individual. If you wish to save the State, you have to abolish the collectivist State ... and return to the Manchester State.[21]

At the Third National Fascist Congress on 8 November 1921, Mussolini would reiterate that when it came to economic matters, fascists were 'declaredly antisocialist', which is to say 'liberal'.[22]

The 'ethical state' was understood as the enemy of the monopolist and bureaucratic state, as a state that reduced its functions to the bare necessities. Mussolini even stressed the need to 'restore the railways and telegraphs to private businesses; because the current apparatus is monstrous and vulnerable in all of its parts'. In Udine, a month before the March, he declared:

> All the trappings of the State collapse like an old operetta stage set when the intimate conviction is lacking that one is carrying out a duty, or better a mission. That is why we want to strip the State of all its economic attributes. Enough with the railwayman State, the postman State, the insurer State. Enough with the State operating at the expenses of all Italian taxpayers and aggravating Italy's exhausted finances.[23]

The justification for this reduction of the state to its repressive and ideological apparatuses was not just pragmatic but idealist: 'Let it not be said that thus emptied out the State remains small. No! It remains a very great thing, because it retains the entire dominion of souls [*spiriti*], while it abdicates the entire dominion of matter.'[24]

Today, as we struggle with fascism's afterlives and repetitions, it helps to remember that it came to power just over one hundred years ago not as a form of 'totalitarianism' fusing the political and the economic, but as a particularly virulent strain of state-led anti-statism. And it was initially welcomed as such by many liberals, from Einaudi to Benedetto Croce. What Mussolini presented as the moral, liberating, problem-solving character of fascism's 'surgical' violence was explicitly articulated in 1921–22 as an anti-democratic violence for the redemption of a nation and state grounded in private accumulation. As he stated at the National Fascist Congress: 'We will absorb liberals and liberalism, because with the method of violence we have buried all preceding methods.'[25]

This promise of liberalism by illiberal means was not the least reason why what brought fascism to power (in 1922 as in 1933) was not ultimately an *insurrection*, but an *invitation* to form a government by sovereign constitutional authorities (King Vittorio Emanuele III, President Paul von Hindenburg). As Daniel Guérin observed in his

Fascism and Big Business, originally published in 1936, here lay the 'vital difference' between socialism and fascism when it came to the seizure of power: the former was the bourgeois state's class enemy, 'while fascism is *in the service of the class* represented by the state' – or at the very least, it was at first embraced and financially supported as such.[26] Contemplating the ravages of neoliberalism-as-civil-war in the early twenty-first century, we should not forget that fascism first came to power in a civil war *for* economic liberalism.

Performing German freedom

In *Libres d'óbeir* (Free to Obey), his study of the Nazi origins of post-war management theories and practices, the French historian Johann Chapoutot has incisively explored a deep seam of National Socialist intellectual production, spearheaded by young jurists, some of them members of the SS, which casts severe doubt on the centrality of the state to the project of racial imperialism (something already noted by Franz Neumann in *Behemoth*, with its pioneering insights into the Nazi 'non-state').[27] For the intellectuals explored by Chapoutot, the state was a counter-selective hindrance to a 'German freedom' understood as a kind of racial spontaneity capable of creating its own immanent right or law.[28] Such freedom could guide the flexible, inventive, target-based 'performances' that officers would carry out in operational liberty and with autonomy regarding their chosen means. German freedom – an old leitmotiv of German nationalism, harking back to a 'freedom of the forests' opposed to dry, abstract, impersonal ('Judeo-Roman') laws – is here the product of a *sui generis* racial withering away of the state that would herald a return to original Germanic models of community beyond individualism, beyond the state and beyond modern sovereignty. As Chapoutot details in *The Law of Blood*:

> According to German positive law as it had existed before 1933, a 'person' was said to be defined by his 'freedom'. [The Nazi jurist

Karl] Larenz denounced this 'freedom' as utterly 'abstract and negative', because it was often presented as protecting the subject from the state and from others. Larenz asserted that freedom was concrete and positive. He argued that rather than being linked to a status, a notion rooted in a static understanding of the law, freedom was a question of position, that of the 'legal position of the individual, who is no longer a person, but a concrete being-member'.[29]

In a seemingly frivolous if no less disturbing register, '*Deutsche Leibeszucht*, the Nazi nudist movement's magazine, argued staunchly that "nudity in nature is not in any way immoral ... Liberated from the shackles imposed on them by civilization and culture", humans could experience 'freedom' and 'health' in all the places nature had to offer.'[30]

This deliberate retrogression was compatible with an overcoming of bureaucratic principles of administration in the direction of a fully *managerial* conception of the exercise of power (and of violence). As Chapoutot recently remarked:

> The National Socialists at least pretended that those people who implemented their ideas were free in their work. Here again we see the image that is essential to Nazi ideology: 'We Germans are free. Over in the East, in the USSR – that's Asia – lived subhumans that were ruled by Jews with a whip. We Germanic people are different, we are free.'[31]

When one of the main Nazi juridical and organisational intellectuals, Reinhard Höhn, came to play such a prominent role in the post-war period, the shift was not so drastic: 'Höhn had the advantage of proposing a management theory with the Harzburg model that was adapted to the spirit of the times. His ideas dominated the German space: "We are free as producers just as we are free as voters or as consumers. We are free, while those over there – under communism – are un-free".'[32]

In the managerial register that, according to Chapoutot, was promoted by the Nazi non-state, 'German freedom' was defined by a performance principle (*Leistungsprinzip*). The individual SS officer was given maximum initiative and flexibility in executing their mission, while the community of the people was defined as a *Leistungsgemeinschaft*, a 'community of achievement'.[33]

The very possibility of a fascist freedom – and the unsettling imperative to reflect on the abiding potentialities of white, settler-colonial, propertied, masculinist figurations of freedom – is excised by the discourse on 'totalitarianism'. This is true even for the latter's most philosophically and historically generative variant, namely Hannah Arendt's *Origins of Totalitarianism*, whose recognition of the boomerang effect of colonialism should have sensitised her to freedom's racial over-determinations.[34] For Arendt, it is definitional that 'totalitarian domination … aims at abolishing freedom, even at eliminating human spontaneity in general, and by no means at a restriction of freedom no matter how tyrannical.'[35] While it certainly speaks to the phenomenology of fascist terror, of the camp, Arendt's notion that totalitarianism – in its logical compulsion and its obliteration of the space for human movement and interaction – is the enemy of spontaneity, of that natal capacity to make a 'new beginning' understood as the very source of freedom, is in the end too comforting. It exempts us from confronting the spontaneities and enjoyments that fascism offers to its managers, militants or minions. If 'freedom as an inner capacity of man is identical with the capacity to begin, just as freedom as a political reality is identical with a space of movement between men', as Arendt suggests, are we sure that fascism is purely and simply freedom's other, its absolute negation?[36]

But if we intend to tackle the twisted nexus of freedom and fascism, we will probably have to probe deeper into the latter's psychic life. In this regard, it is perhaps telling that an effort to depict the 'psychology of Nazism' as the veritable apotheosis of a centuries-long 'escape from freedom', the titular concept of Erich Fromm's wartime book, also contains a reflection on what appears

to be a very contemporary psycho-social type, *the authoritarian rebel*.
For Fromm, such rebels

> look like persons who, on the basis of their inner strength and integ-
> rity, fight those forces that block their freedom and independence.
> However, the authoritarian character's fight against authority is
> essentially defiance. It is an attempt to assert himself and to overcome
> his own feeling of powerlessness by fighting authority, although the
> longing for submission remains present, whether consciously or
> unconsciously. The authoritarian character is never a 'revolution-
> ary'; I should like to call him a 'rebel'. There are many individuals
> and political movements that are puzzling to the superficial observer
> because of what seems to be an inexplicable change from 'radical-
> ism' to extreme authoritarianism. Psychologically, these people are
> the typical 'rebels' ... The authoritarian character loves those con-
> ditions that limit human freedom, he loves being submitted to fate.[37]

Is the fascist love of freedom simply a detour on the way to submission – what Marcuse termed not freedom but 'acquiescent
license'?[38] This is a question that I think anti-fascist theory still
needs to meditate on, not least as a moment in the clarification of
its own philosophy of liberation.

Non-states and anti-states: between fascism and neoliberalism

In spite of, but in a sense also *because* of, its paeans to the total
state, fascism could be understood as the simultaneous intensification
and dismantling of the modern figure of the state. Not a Hobbe-
sian Leviathan, but, to borrow the title of Neumann's pioneering
analysis of the Nazi non-state, a Behemoth – an unstable, polycratic
agency of racial imperialism that accelerates the social contradictions of monopoly capitalism in 'a form of society where direct
domination over the population takes place, a domination based

upon the negation of the mediations deriving from the existence of a relatively independent and stable authority like the state'; 'an irrational, chaotic, lawless anarchic condition of domination, without a coherent political theory, a non-state that forcibly kept the economy going for the power accumulation of a leader and the profit of the large industrial capitalists'.[39] It is no accident that Neumann forged his analysis in ideological battle with his former interlocutor Carl Schmitt who, in his 1933 *Staat, Bewegung, Volk* (State, Movement, People), had sought to lend doctrinal form to this sublation of the independence of the state by the *Führerprinzip* and its ontology of race and force – while disavowing the capitalist gangsterism and racketeering that Neumann so pitilessly details. Neumann's close friend Herbert Marcuse echoed these insights – in the process countering the thesis shared by their fellow Institute for Social Research members Friedrich Pollock and Max Horkheimer, according to whom Nazism had spawned a historically new and potentially stable form of authoritarian state capitalism.

For Marcuse, Nazism had effectively abolished the distinction between state and society on which the concept of the former depended, leading to a volatile situation based on the 'direct and immediate self-government by the prevailing social groups over the rest of the population' – a *de facto* abolition not just of the modern figure of the state but of modern law, which Marcuse finds legitimated and mystified in Schmitt's argument for a 'plurality of orders' rescinding any even notional transcendence of the juridical. Though one may still wish to speak of totalitarianism here, there was no such thing as a *totalitarian state* in a situation dominated by the threefold sovereignty of capital, party and army and in which Hitler operated as a locus of compromise – the state thus becoming merely 'the government of hypostatised economic, social and political forces'. Not a totalitarian state but a *machine-state*, whose performance is measured by its efficiency.[40]

For Marcuse, the machine-state here 'seems to move by its own necessity and is still flexible and obedient to the slightest change in the set-up of the ruling groups. All human relations are absorbed by the objective wheelwork of control and expansion.'[41] Rather than echoing the rather undialectical juxtaposition between market society and totalitarianism that some members of the Frankfurt School in exile were articulating at the time, Marcuse pointed to the complex genetic and structural relation between fascism and liberal capitalism – something he had already begun to sketch out in the 1934 essay on 'The Struggle Against Liberalism in the Totalitarian View of the State', where he also cited Ludwig von Mises's notorious reference in his 1927 *Liberalism* to fascism as a saviour of Western civilisation, albeit an 'emergency makeshift' to be supplanted by a fortified liberal order.[42] As Marcuse declared in 1942:

> The emergence of the Third Reich is the emergence of the most efficient and ruthless competitor. The National Socialist state is not the reversal but the consummation of competitive individualism. The regime releases all those forces of brutal self-interest which the democratic countries have tried to curb and combine with the interest of freedom. Like any other form of individualist society, National Socialism operates on the basis of private ownership in the means of production. Accordingly, it is made up by two polar strata, the small number of those who control the productive process and the bulk of the population which, directly or indirectly, is dependent upon the former. Under National Socialism it is the status of the individual in this latter stratum that has most drastically changed. Here, too, however, the changes bring to fruition rather than contradict certain tendencies of individualist society.[43]

Together with our brief excavation of Italian fascism's early self-image as a violent nationalism aiming to impose economic liberalism, this understanding of Nazi Germany as a 'non-state' – the volatile arena for political and economic power-competitions, driven and legitimated by racial imperialism – should help to erode our unexamined reliance on a totalitarianism paradigm that treats fascism and liberalism as simple antonyms. Fascism is not fully and adequately grasped as a *statolatry*, nor as the subsumption of markets under the state. Liberalism, for its part, is only identified with the limitation of state and political power at the cost of evacuating its historical reality.[44]

What about the notion that neoliberalism can be adequately grasped as *state phobia*, as an economic war machine set on the dismantling of state capacities? This useful fable has been amply dispelled by all serious recent research on the intellectual and political history of neoliberalism. In their powerful polemical history of neoliberalism, *Le choix de la guerre civile* (The Choice of Civil War), Pierre Dardot, Haud Guéguen, Christian Laval and Pierre Sauvêtre encapsulate this position with trenchant clarity: as their history chronicles, from Santiago de Chile to Maastricht, Brasilia to Washington, DC, '*there is no neoliberalism other than an authoritarian one*', since at its core lies the 'sovereignty of private right guaranteed by a strong power' – a strong state for a free market. This constitutively implies 'a political project of the neutralisation of socialism in all its forms and, beyond this, of all the forms of a demand for equality, a project borne by theorists and essayists who are also, from the start, *political entrepreneurs*'. To this end, 'the neoliberal social construction restructures State/society relations, not with the aim of weakening the state, but rather with that of reinforcing state institutions which create and fortify the disciplinary power of markets.'[45]

But if we wish to attend to the fascist potentials in neoliberalism, it is imperative to attend to analyses that foreground the shaping function of race and racism in the development and implantation of neoliberal policies and ideology. To be more precise, I think we can say that focusing on neoliberalism's racial regimes provides incomparable evidence for the thesis that it enacts a *differential* reinforcement of the state, which in turn compounds and refunctions those 'fatal couplings of power and difference' that, according to Stuart Hall, define the making, unmaking and remaking of race.[46] In this regard, I think that much is to be gained by exploring a

conceptual and analytical formula advanced by Ruth Wilson Gilmore
in the ambit of her ongoing political and geographical investigation
of the nexus of state capacities, class warfare and racialisation in the
'prison-industrial complex' – the *anti-state state*.[47] In a 2008 essay
co-authored with Craig Gilmore, 'Restating the Obvious', Gilmore
provides us with some key elements for a materialist analysis of the
place of the state in the reactionary political cycle in which we find
ourselves. I'd like briefly to itemise three of them here, in view of
suggesting their usefulness as tools with which to think the present
and its fascist potentials.

First, an analytical distinction between state and government.
A state is here defined as 'a territorially bounded set of relatively
specialised institutions that develop and change over time in the
gaps and fissures of social conflict, compromise, and cooperation',
while governments are 'the animating forces – policies plus personnel – that put state capacities into motion and orchestrate or
coerce people in their jurisdictions to conduct their lives according
to centrally made and enforced rules'.[48] The state is fundamentally understood in terms of capacities, that is, materially enacted
and enforceable powers – to distribute or hierarchise, develop or
abandon, care or criminalise. One of the chief aims of neoliberalism
(especially in its overweening obsession with the constitutionalisation of the market order) is to 'bake in' its principles into these state
capacities themselves, so that even a nominally socialist or social-
democratic government will still be compelled to carry out neoliberal
policies.

Second, in polities structured by the long legacies and mutable
regimes of racial capitalism, the state is also a racial state, one that
may well operate administratively and juridically through a manifest commitment to 'colour-blindness'. As the Gilmores write, in a
passage that ably encapsulates the virtues of a historical-materialist
geographical sensibility when it comes to the nexus of politics
and race:

The state's management of racial categories is analogous to the management of highways or ports or telecommunication: racist ideological and material practices are infrastructure that needs to be updated, upgraded, and modernized periodically: this is what is meant by racialization. And the state itself, not just interests or forces external to the state, is built and enhanced through these practices. Sometimes these practices result in 'protecting' certain racial groups, and other times they result in sacrificing them.[49]

Third, while the state has of course been an integral material and symbolic partner across the history of capitalism, the present has come to be defined by a singular *rhetoric* – bound to the trajectory of neoliberalism but also exceeding it – namely that of the anti-state state, a state that promises its own demise and which employs that promise to increase, intensify and differentiate its capacities, its powers. The combative version – think Ronald Reagan's dictum: 'The nine most terrifying words in the English language are: I'm from the Government, and I'm here to help' – is doubled by fatalistic academic apologia; recall the tired mantras of 'globalisation' as the eclipse of the state. By contrast with a vision of mass incarceration as the outcome of a drive to privatise, the extraordinary, racialised growth in prisons is internal to and emblematic of transmutations in the state, in the composition of its agents and resources, which a one-dimensional understanding of neoliberalism – a 'low-flying economism', to borrow Stuart Hall's quip – often obscures. As the Gilmores note:

> Because prisons and prisoners are part of the structure of the state, they enable governments to establish state legitimacy through a claim to provide social 'protection' combined with their monopoly on the delegation of violence. The state establishes legitimacy precisely *because* it violently dominates certain people and thereby defines them (and makes them visible to others) as the sort of people who should be pushed around. In modelling behaviour for the polity, the anti-state state naturalizes violent domination.[50]

In articulating the entanglement of the prison-industrial complex with the anti-state state as 'a state that grows on the promise of shrinking', the Gilmores link back to Antonio Negri's pioneering analyses of the *crisis state*, and especially to his incisive contention that:

> The counter-revolution of the capitalist entrepreneur today can only operate strictly within the context of an increase in the coercive powers of the state. The 'new right' ideology of laissez-faire implies as its corollary the extension of new techniques of coercive and state intervention in society at large.[51]

But what Negri's vantage point – that of the mass mobilisations and creeping civil war in Italy in the 1970s – may not have fully equipped him to grasp, and what we need to dwell on to discern the fascist potentials in the anti-state state, are those subjective investments in the naturalisations of violent mastery that go together with the promotion of possessive and racialised conceptions of freedom. Here we need to reflect not just on the fact that neoliberalism operates through a racial state, or that, as commentators have begun to recognise and detail, it is shaped by a racist and civilisational imaginary that delimits *who* is capable of market freedoms.[52] We must also attend to the fact that the anti-state state could became an object of popular attachment or better, populist investment, only through the mediation of race.

In his germinal analyses of Thatcherism, Stuart Hall demonstrated – in ways still profoundly pertinent to our moment – how authoritarian populism gestated in the 1960s and 1970s around a concatenation of racialised moral panics. This process played a key mediating, consolidating and reproducing function for the rise of neoliberalism to political pre-eminence. Racism was in this sense a kind of internal supplement to neoliberalism. In Hall's Gramscian terminology, it made it possible (under the specific conditions of a crisis-wracked England) to neutralise 'the contradiction between

the people and the state/power bloc and [to win] popular interpellations so decisively for the Right'.[53] Authoritarian populism could
accordingly be understood as

> the project, central to the politics of Thatcherism to ground neo-
> liberal politics directly in an appeal to 'the people'; to root them in
> the essentialist categories of common-sense experience and practi-
> cal moralism – and this to construct, not simply awaken, classes,
> groups and interests into a particular definition of 'the people'.[54]

This construction was and remains racialised – by successive figurations of the non- or un-people (in the UK, from young Black
proletarians figured as 'muggers' to Muslims on a path to 'radicalisation' to, most recently, Eastern European workers threatening
'British jobs'). In its English variant, neoliberalism in power was first
articulated as a national populism (and, in the Falklands venture, a
regenerated *social imperialism*), and such it largely remains. Whence
the critical function of vanishing mediators such as Enoch Powell,
whose more overt and combative racist rhetoric seeded a more
capacious successor (a dynamic paralleled by the relation between
Goldwater and Nixon in the US context, or the role of the Front
National in accelerating the rightward drift of mainstream French
politics).

For Hall, the ideological crusade of the mid-1970s – Negri's
counter-revolution of the capitalist entrepreneur – required penetration into 'some of the core and root social ideas in the population',
and the staging of a kind of popular 'ventriloquism' that could
draw on the 'real material sources of popular discontent', securing
the people to the practices of the dominant bloc and drawing on
the 'massively conservative force' of 'traditional and uncorrected
common sense'. In this respect, by contrast with its social-democratic
(Labour) antecedent, this authoritarian populist neoliberalism
effected a kind of passive revolution grounded in 'unceasing efforts
to construct the movement towards a more authoritarian regime

from a massive populist base'. In other words, neoliberalism must be populist because it cannot be popular-democratic.[55]

Hall, as we briefly saw in our discussion of racial fascism, was foregrounding the specificity of Thatcherism by way of critical contrast with a facile leftist stance that flattened all authoritarianism onto a familiar fascist spectre – a lesson that remains valid today. Yet it is not irrelevant to ask how a neoliberalism that entered power as a nationalist or indeed neo-imperialist populism, instrumentalising racist moral panics and racialised (and gendered) class struggles, also prepared the contemporary resurgence of a far right that remains based on 'not the reversal but the consummation of competitive individualism'.[56] As evidenced in US, UK, Brazilian, German and other scenarios, there are no *cordons sanitaires* between combative neoliberalisms and the multiple variants of contemporary reaction, including neo- or post-fascist ones. It is useful to recall here the contention of Dardot et al. that neoliberalism 'cannot be positively defined by a *specific political regime*':

> Here lies the *heart* of the authoritarian dimension of neoliberal politics: the structure of the state may vary, the political personnel and its behaviour too, what is essential is that those in government be sufficiently strong to impose the constitutionalisation of private right and thus restrict the field of what can be deliberated upon.[57]

Whether a revanchist right-wing populism may, wittingly or otherwise, threaten that constitutionalisation is not clear – even today's protectionist gestures mostly respect the boundary conditions of neoliberalism and its class imperatives. Perhaps rather than these doctrinal issues – often blurred by the ideological flexibility and opportunism of the right – we should attend to the social and political trajectories that bind the possibilities of fascist resurgence to neoliberalism's morbid symptoms.

Here it is useful to recall Grégoire Chamayou's recent analysis of the European birth of 'authoritarian liberalism' in the fateful year of 1932 and its unsettling resonances with the present, namely in what he calls

> the austerian-authoritarian mechanism [*engrenage*]: the socially dis-
> astrous effects of [the government's] rejected economic programme
> sapped the threadbare political basis on which it could still rely, so
> that it soon could not continue in the same direction, save by going
> up a notch in its authoritarianism in order to impose measures of
> the same kind that produced the same genre of effects, and so on.[58]

Not only does the anti-state state manifest itself as 'a series of punitive responses to the chaos it has facilitated', but, as Ugo Palheta
has compellingly shown for the French case, the protracted crises
of hegemony and social reproduction effected by neoliberal policies
have contributed to the flourishing of fascist potentials.[59] The 2007–8
crisis was a special moment in this respect, in France and elsewhere,
revealing that neoliberalism is unable to generate socially acceptable solutions, that all it can offer is a seemingly endless horizon of
austerity, stagnation, declining living standards, increasing inequality, accumulation by dispossession, organised abandonment and a
repressive hardening of the state against any challenge or alternative.
The recombinations of neoliberalism manifest the hardening of
authoritarian tendencies, in a context of domination without hegemony in which the ruling classes undergo a process of radicalisation,
a context in which their continued supremacy is dependent on a
hollowing out of democratic rights and capacities.

Here it is difficult not to recall Karl Polanyi's dictum that 'in
order to comprehend German fascism, we must revert to Ricardian
England' and his related observation according to which fascism was
'merely the outcome of the mutual incompatibility of Democracy and
Capitalism in our time'. Fascism, for the author of *The Great Transformation*, is 'that revolutionary solution which keeps Capitalism
untouched'.[60] Behind this lay the thesis of a longue durée of fascist
potentials, grounded in the 'recrudescence of the old hostility of

capitalism to popular government'.[61] Ruthless hostility to a substantive, socio-economic notion of democracy, such as Polanyi's, is not simply something that the anti-state state, as rhetoric and practice of neoliberalism, shares with the new faces of reaction. Neoliberalism's racialised anti-democratic animus creates the material and ideological conditions for efforts to win popular interpellations for the far right, in the electoral arena and beyond.[62] The modality through which fascist potentials or trajectories emerge out of neoliberalism's 'disruptive strains' involves the turbocharging of inherent traits of the neoliberal order – spoliation of nature for the sake of profit, attacks on the distribution of the social wage, glorification of possessive individualism and predatory entrepreneurialism – under the cover of a challenge to some of its supposedly defining dimensions.[63] The anti-statism of contemporary reaction marries culture war themes and corporate diktats, especially those of fossil capital – think Steve Bannon's infamous call for the 'deconstruction of the administrative state'.[64]

Today's far right melds a cynically selective anti-statism with a revanchist ethno-nationalism passionately attached to the symbolism and reality of the repressive state – think of the 'thin blue line' American flag, 'blue lives matter' slogans, and the like. Late fascism is thus both a reaction against certain facets of the neoliberal moment (those that come to be coded and sometimes racialised as 'globalist') and a passionate over-identification with the coercive dimensions of the anti-state state. It brings into the open neoliberalism's disavowed reliance on civilisational narratives of white superiority, while prolonging its contradictory modernisation and repair of the infrastructure of the racial state. This late fascism, coming *after* hollow prophecies about the neoliberal neutralisation of the political, is a kind of second-order or reflexive affirmation of neoliberalism's authoritarian underside. It is sustained by the blurring of the borders between liberal conceptions of freedom and individualism (as market freedom, freedom to own, freedom from interference with individual sovereignty) and what we could term fascist visions of freedom (freedom to dominate, to rule) – both drawn to aggressive imaginaries of competition or 'fitness' and a repulsion for solidarity, care, vulnerability.

Those whose horizon remains that of the root-and-branch transformation of the state understood as a condensation and vehicle of class power and social violence – who aim, as communists, at a 'non-state state' – will thus have to contend with the embedding of fascist potentials within the anti-state state. Such potentials may, in times of crisis, organise themselves around new forms of that exterminationist and entrepreneurial violence that defined the Nazi Behemoth as a *non-state*.

4
A Phantom with Limbs of Steel

Whoever is not willing to talk about capitalism should also keep
quiet about fascism.

— Max Horkheimer, 'The Jews and Europe' (1939)

Blood rises up against formal understanding, race against the rational
pursuit of ends, honor against profit, bonds against the caprice that
is called 'freedom', organic totality against individualistic dissolution, valor against bourgeois security, politics against the primacy
of the economy, state against society, *Volk* against the individual and
the mass.

— Ernst Krieck, *Nationalpolitische Erziehung* (1933)[1]

Fascism and real abstraction

Having explored fascist visions of freedom and their overt entanglements and unspoken affinities with varieties of liberalism and
neoliberalism, we still need to contend with the images of capital
that condition fascist politics. As I argue in this chapter, fascism's
relation to capitalism is best investigated in terms of its struggles
with economic, juridical and political abstractions.

Where some critics have seen in fascism a passion for abstractions, others have diagnosed a phobia of the abstract as one of its leading traits. These perspectives are not necessarily incompatible. The Vichy collaborationist regime in wartime France, for instance, substituted the revolutionary universalism of *liberté, égalité, fraternité* with *travail, famille, patrie* – freedom was supplanted by work, equality by the family, fraternity by fatherland. As Alain Badiou has observed: 'Fascisms invariably replaced the subjective universality of truth procedures (political invention, artistic creation, and so on), which they detested, with the designation of great referential collectives: the nation, the race, the West.'[2] As we saw in the previous chapter, the 'same' abstract idea, freedom, can be stripped of its 'subjective universality' and ascribed to one of these collectives ('German Freedom'), or stripped of any of its emancipatory content ('freedom to obey'). But to capture fascism's ambiguous relation to abstraction, it does not suffice to explore its relation to abstract political entities and signifiers. We also need to delve into fascism's reactive relationship to capital's 'real abstractions', a relationship that crystallises in the racial frameworks of romantic anti-capitalism.[3] In the next chapter, we will build upon these arguments to explore the link between capital's social forms and the temporalities of fascism.

While the most dogged theorist of real abstraction, namely the German Marxist philosopher Alfred Sohn-Rethel, made an important contribution to the empirical study of the nexus between fascism and capitalism, the theoretical development of the articulation between fascism and real abstraction is principally to be sought at the margins of the oeuvre of his only true philosophical interlocutor, Theodor W. Adorno, and in the largely neglected theory of fascist ideology sketched out by Norbert Guterman and Henri Lefebvre in their 1936 book *La conscience mystifiée* (Mystified Consciousness).[4] Before exploring these theoretical threads, we need to account for the centrality of the phobia of abstraction in fascist and, more specifically, Nazi ideology. As we will see, fascism's fear and loathing of the abstract knots together capital, law and race, while its democratic afterlives can also be understood as pathologies of capitalist abstraction.

Making abstraction Jewish

In *The Law of Blood: Thinking and Acting as a Nazi*, Johann Chapoutot has surveyed the National Socialist response to the cumulative 'alienations' and 'denaturations' enacted by Christianity, that 'Judeo-Asiatic theory of salvation' that for the Nazis went hand-in-hand with the usurpation of the tellurian roots of German justice by the 'Judeo-Roman' apparatus of abstract law (complementing the whole conspiratorial complex of 'Judeo-Bolshevism', which linked the revolutionary abstractions of communism to Jewish nomadism, cosmopolitanism and subversion).[5] The alienation of the German *Volk* is understood by National Socialist ideologues as the supplanting of the natural, rooted morality of *right*, the expression of a vital and racial normativity, by a multitude of abstract *laws*.[6] This was the perspective that dictated the nineteenth among the twenty-five points of the NSDAP's 1920 programme: 'We demand substitution of a German common law in place of the Roman Law serving a materialistic world-order.'

Summarising the ideological *Weltanschauung* advanced by Nazi jurists and legal historians, Chapoutot writes that for them,

> Jews were beings of abstraction, for they hated what was real. This hatred had led them to invent artifice, to take refuge in what did not exist, in phantasmagoria confabulated in their poor sick heads. It was the Jews who had written the laws: they were the 'people of the Law' because they were incapable of living and thinking the law – the natural law, that is, which was the pure expression of the natural world they were defying.[7]

Manifesting that symptomatic weaponisation of contradictions that is so rife in fascist ideology, the purported Jewish drive towards abstraction was 'biologically' explained by their being so racially mixed that they constituted a non-race (*Unrasse*) or counter-race (*Gegenrasse*). With lethal mimetic irony, the incoherence of racist ideology is projected into the putatively unnatural substance of its target, which is in turn represented as contradictory *because* it is impure, but also seeking shelter and stability in abstract formality and normativity as antidotes to an absence of stable substance. Presenting at the 1936 conference on 'Jewishness in the Science of Right', Carl Schmitt would crystallise this argument that the mixed ontology of the Jew ('Jewish chaos', in his terms) requires a counterweight at the juridical and epistemological level (in 'Jewish legality'), thus marrying 'a crudely materialist sensualism and the most abstract moralism'.[8] As Chapoutot summarises this line of racist thought:

> This formlessness had led the Jews to seek refuge in formalism: since their ontology was labile and uncertain, they found reassurance and structure in and through the rigidity of unquestioned and imperative norms. The Jews were the people of the law because they needed its normative backbone to live. This law did not lead them to construct a cosmos, however; instead it commanded them to act in keeping with its nature, which was to sow chaos and devastation. Formless, deformed, the Jew deformed and destroyed, unlike the Aryan, who informed and conformed. Seen in this light, the need to rid German legal life of all Jewish elements was understandable. The Jewish mind had to be hunted down, and practitioners of Judaism mercilessly expelled.[9]

This formalist formlessness begins with the imposition of what Nazi jurists viewed as a 'Judaised' Roman law. Summarising the principles of the National Socialist juridical outlook in 1934, Schmitt would articulate Nazism as a critique of separation, its great deed the 'overcoming of the schism and shearing that stood in the service of certain political tendencies for many centuries'. Against this 'entire system of antitheses', these 'systematic shearings' – 'body and soul, spirit and material, law and politics, law and economy, law and morality' – what was needed was a recognition of the fact that (quoting an anonymous US legal scholar): 'We are today experiencing the bankruptcy of the *idées générales*.' The Nazi legal movement was thus tasked with undoing 'the monopoly of the juridical' and tearing down a 'normativistic tower of Babel and put[ting] in its place a healthy, concrete order of thought'. It was therefore necessary for Schmitt to recognise the ongoing aftereffects of 'a certain legal-historical event, namely the *reception of Roman law*', which, while beginning in the concrete forms of life of Roman peasants, *paterfamilias* and soldiers, 'becomes the most senseless, most scandalous, most dangerous thing in the world once detached from a concrete reality, carried over to another order of a *Volk*, once the abstraction of its detached maxims is passed off as the only pure juridical and scholarly wisdom'. This danger will become glaringly manifest in the solidarity between the juridical abstractions of Roman law and the 'ideological-abstract-ghostlike monism' advanced by Soviet communism. Crucial to the corruption that marks the reception of Roman law, according to Schmitt, is the mediation of the 'existentially normative' Jewish people, who, as eternal *metics*, require a 'calculably effective norm' abstracted from the concrete. As Schmitt puts it, pithily and xenophobically: 'The foreigner wants to have a timetable to know when and where he can get off. As a result, he puts in place of justice the law in the sense of the previously determined, calculable norm.' Political anti-Semitism and the 'struggle against Roman law' thus turn out to have a more than elective affinity. With the rise of a 'concrete order of thought' over against an 'abstract-normativistic' one, German jurists will have to choose and 'it will do them no good to retreat onto the melting sheet of ice of the old forms of convulsive normativism and positivism'.[10]

The modern march of formless formalism against racial concreteness is further exacerbated from the perspective of a Nazi critique of abstraction by the French Revolution, which is figured as a kind of race war that hunted down aristocratic (and *a fortiori* Germanic, Aryan) purity, replacing it with the amorphous, the undefined, the hybrid. Monetary and financial abstraction are themselves envisaged as allies of this long revolution of the formless.[11] For the Nazi philosopher Alfred Rosenberg, speaking during the occupation of Paris, the war against England was a war between blood and gold, understood 'as a financial instrument – as a quantitative, democratic, universal equaliser that dissolved all hierarchies, especially those of race and blood'.[12] According to the Nazi historian of legal philosophy Kurt Schilling, the mania for abstraction could be traced all the way back to the Stoics in Ancient Greece, through to Rousseau and the Enlightenment-era rise of an age of quantification and a mathematical democracy grounded on an abstraction hostile to life.[13] The Italian philosopher and occultist Julius Evola, writing in the journal *Difesa della razza* (In Defence of Race), would similarly argue for the juxtaposition between the 'Jewish inclination towards mathematical abstraction' and an ancient Aryan vision of existence, steeped in a cosmic and solar *Weltanschauung*.[14] The opposition between the mathematics of equality and the biology of difference was also advanced by the jurist Gustav Adolf Walz, for whom the primacy of logic always hid a biological failure or a secret political messianism, itself chalked up to a racial causality. Ultimately, the modern epoch was to be grasped as a cultural and intellectual war of annihilation against the Nordic race in which Roman law, natural right, economic liberalism, individualism and capitalism were in alliance (and capitalism would ultimately join hands with communism in a war of abstract universalism against national-racial concreteness).

This spurious war on abstraction was vivisected in the 'Research Project on Anti-Semitism' published in the final 1941, English-language volume of the Institute's *Zeitschrift für Sozialforschung/ Studies in Philosophy and Social Science* – the targeting of Schmitt's juridical Judeophobia being no surprise, considering not just Schmitt's intellectual prominence but the fact that an Institute member, Otto Kirchheimer, had studied under him.[15] Instead of purely repudiating anti-Semitism as manipulation or prejudice, the Institute sought to detail how certain Jewish social character traits identified, magnified and distorted by the anti-Semite 'find their roots in the economic life of the Jew, in his particular function in society and in the consequences of his economic activity'. The first is the notion that Jews do the 'dirty' if immaterial work of capital, namely in their function as 'middlemen'. What we encounter here is a critical ingredient of any historically informed theory of intra-European 'racial capitalism', one that is absent from Cedric Robinson's pioneering treatment in *Black Marxism*, just as, conversely, the profound links between the racialisation of Islam, anti-Black racisms and anti-Semitism receive scant attention in the writings of the Frankfurt School.

As the 'Research Project' notes, 'from olden times the practice of extending credit has prevented the antagonism between the possessors of power and the economically oppressed population from leading to recurrent catastrophes', but in crisis the Jew becomes the perceived factor of impoverishment.[16] The increasing importance of intermediary functions to modern capital is then the basis for the 'maneuver of distraction' that presents an intrinsically Jewish 'non-productive capital' as the source of social ills. Emblematic of this operation is the imaginary world of Richard Wagner's *Ring*, which 'contrasts the heroic productive Siegfried, a mixture of the munition manufacturer, the condottiere, and the rowdy, with the dwarf, a symbol of the owners, merchants, and the resentful, eternally complaining proletariat'. The Nazi struggle against Roman law is then traced back to the political economy of Jewish life under capitalism and its ideological effects:

> Since its Roman origin, civil law has been the law of creditors. Whereas it recognizes no difference between any groups or individuals but aims at the universal protection of property, it is a priori antagonistic to the debtor. Historically, because of the creditor role of the Jews, deriving from their functions as bankers and merchants,

we find them usually on the side of Rational law. Their foes, on the other hand, favor a vague natural law based on the 'sound instinct of the people'.[17]

This affiliation with juridical abstraction, grounded in the historical trends determining the social positioning of certain Jews within the ambit of European racial capitalism, is then presented as the further basis for the association of Jews with abstract intellectual labour *tout court*.[18] The 'Research Project' was, among other things, an effort to ground the anti-Semitic fascist phobia for abstraction in the distorted refraction of certain real social processes in the history of European racial capitalism. What's more, it drew on historical materialist method to blast an emancipatory core out of the lethal stereotype of the Jew as the bearer of life-denying abstraction:

> The psychological faculty of abstraction developed with the com-
> mercial and financial function. In the commodity economy, men
> face each other as equals, not according to distinctions of birth or
> religion. It does not matter who they are, but only what commod-
> ity they want to buy or sell. The abstract notion of the thing as a
> commodity corresponds to the abstract notion of man. It makes no
> difference if one sells art objects, cotton or guns ... Even if one
> assumes that 'rationalism' is the main trend among Jews, one has no
> reason whatsoever to bow to the verdict which anti-Semites reach
> on the basis of that assumption. The levelling that results from
> abstract thinking is a prerequisite for the development of the world,
> in a truly human sense, for this type of thinking divests human rela-
> tionships and things of their taboos and brings them into the realm
> of reason. Jews have therefore always stood in the front ranks of
> the struggle for democracy and freedom. The study of the so-called
> Jewish mentality explains why the Jews are blamed simultaneously
> for capitalistic and revolutionary relativistic and dogmatic, tolerant
> and intolerant 'mindedness'. Such contradictory accusations do not
> in fact reflect upon the Jews but rather upon the state of mankind

in the present historical period. The Jews are but the bearers of society's inconsistencies.[19]

In moving to the place of anti-Semitism within Nazi ideology itself, the 'Research Project' seeks to ground the very possibility of Nazi policies against the Jews in the political-economic shift out of a market economy, the delinking of German capitalism from the anonymous abstract and impersonal compulsions of the market.[20] This thesis will chime with a broader, and problematic, set of arguments that link the market economy and liberal ideology to bourgeois individualism, something that the Frankfurt School is sometimes uncertain whether to desperately try and retain or to usher into oblivion. As the 'Research Project' argues, in a section entitled 'The Change in the Function of Money':

> In a laissez faire economy the entrepreneur could tell by the increase or decrease of the money capital which he invested in an undertaking, the extent to which it was useful to society. If a factory or any other business could not keep pace with general economic developments, this was expressed in its financial statements and finally in the disappearance of the undertaking itself ... In the totalitarian state the free market is abolished, and the ability of money to 'declare' ceases to exist ... The market, an anonymous and democratic tribunal, is replaced by the command and plan of those in power ... The decline in importance of the spheres of economic activity in which the German Jews were chiefly engaged is the basis of their becoming superfluous. Their economic existence was intimately connected with the liberal system of economy and with its judicial and political conditions. In liberalism ... the unfit are eliminated by the effectiveness of the mechanism of competition, no matter what their names are or what personal qualities they have. In the totalitarian system, however, individuals or entire social groups can be sent to the gallows at any moment for political or other reasons. The replacement of the market by a planned economy of the state

bureaucracy and the decline of the power of money capital makes possible the policy against the Jews in the Third Reich.[21]

Here as elsewhere in the work of the Institute for Social Research in exile (as well as after its return to Frankfurt), the link between the commodity abstraction and the political and juridical ('democratic') abstraction of the citizen or person is at times articulated in a manner that remains on the hither side of Marx's articulation of this relationship in 'On the Jewish Question'.[22] This is, for instance, the case when Adorno, in his 'Remarks on *The Authoritarian Personality*', speaks of 'the decay of individuality brought about by the decline of free competition and market economy'.[23] What this suggests is a far too linear conception of the relation between the monetary abstraction and the abstraction of the bourgeois citizen-subject. In the process, the whole question of fascism's relation to racial capitalism is rendered opaque by an undialectical distinction between the economic violence of the market ('the unfit are eliminated by the effectiveness of the mechanism of competition') and the political violence of the totalitarian state, as though racialisation were absent under market rule and capitalist compulsions lacking in Nazi racial imperialism. Notwithstanding the profound limitations of this contrast between liberalism and totalitarianism, the writings of the Institute remain instructive in their effort to pose the problem of the nexus between the historically shifting modalities of capitalist abstraction, on the one hand, and the political forms of domination and racialisation, on the other.

The stereopath

What of the relation between abstraction and the *potential for* rather than *actuality of* fascism? This question is addressed especially in Adorno's qualitative analyses from *The Authoritarian Personality*, specifically in a section of that massive collective study entitled 'Ticket Thinking and Personalization in Politics'. Adorno was trying to excavate the threads linking ignorance and confusion in political matters with the objective social grounds for a psychological disposition to fascism. The problem is very much of the kind that would later be christened 'cognitive mapping' by Fredric Jameson, namely that of the (im)possibility of generating a situational representation of one's relations to capital as totality.[24]

Adorno frames fascism in terms of the individual's scalar, epistemological and material alienation from the dynamics and levers of capitalist power. It is at this level that Adorno places the emergence of 'certain techniques of orientation' to cope with the paralysing anxieties generated by the abstract opacity that pertains to modern capitalism, the need to generate 'substitutes for knowledge'. These cognitive surrogates take two polar but specular forms, a misplaced abstractness that goes by the name of *stereotypy* (which Adorno sees as at once a tool and a scar) and a misplaced concreteness in the guise of personalisation. Underlying these techniques is the objective social drift towards an integral standardisation or reification of social life – the same one that is thematised in Adorno's concurrent studies of 'commodity listening' and 'plugging' in popular music and his polemics against the appearance of freedom and improvisation that defines the 'jazz subject'.

It is the largely achieved tendency towards integral reification that makes the method of *The Authoritarian Personality* possible, since the social and the psychological ultimately collapse in the obsolescence of bourgeois individuality and autonomy, the end of 'experience' properly so-called. This is the situation in which the 'more stereotyped life itself becomes the more the stereopath feels in the right, sees his frame of thinking vindicated by reality'.[25] Mimicking the very coldness and alienness of the society that triggered anxiety in the first place, stereotypy and stereopathy direct the subject towards a kind of ersatz concreteness. They promote personalisation defined as

the tendency to describe objective social and economic processes, political programs, internal and external tendencies in terms of some person identified with the case in question rather than taking the trouble to perform the impersonal intellectual operations required by the abstractness of the social processes themselves.[26]

In sum:

> Stereotypy misses reality in so far as it dodges the concrete and contents itself with preconceived, rigid, and overgeneralized ideas to which the individual attributes a kind of magical omnipotence. Conversely, personalization dodges the real abstractness, that is to say, the 'reification' of social reality which is determined by property relations and in which the human beings themselves are, as it were, mere appendages. Stereotypy and personalization are two divergent parts of an actually nonexperienced world.[27]

It is somewhat perplexing that Adorno characterises these poles as 'irreconcilable', if we reflect on the way in which racist thought in general, and anti-Semitism in particular, as stigmatising *personalisations of abstraction*, operate a powerful synthesis of these false compasses for a reified society.[28] In late fascism, stereotypy and personalisation converge, aided and abetted by algorithmic architectures.[29]

Fascism's democratic survivals

Adorno took on the problem of fascist potentials again after his return to Frankfurt. This mainly involved reflecting theoretically on the *Gruppenexperiment* carried out with Pollock and others to empirically research German perceptions of war guilt.[30] The notion of real abstraction reared its head again, now as a kind of explanation for the afterlives of fascism. In a famous lecture first delivered in 1959, 'The Meaning of Working Through the Past', Adorno declared that he considered 'the survival of National Socialism within democracy to be potentially more menacing than the survival of fascist tendencies against democracy'.[31] The persistence of fascist tendencies in the guise of forgetting was not a matter of German psychopathology, but of a specifically capitalist social structure and social unconscious. The atrophy of historical consciousness that made the living on of Hitlerism possible, Adorno declared,

> is necessarily connected to the advancement of the bourgeois principle. Bourgeois society is universally situated under the law of exchange, of the like-for-like of accounts that match and that leave no remainder. In its very essence exchange is something timeless; like *ratio* itself, like the operations of mathematics according to their pure form, they remove the aspect of time.[32]

The persistence of fascism within democracy is thus a matter of capitalism's real abstractions, as mediated by mass psychology. For Adorno, there is an intimate solidarity between the internalisation of incapacity transmitted by a dominant individualist ideology and the compensatory collective fantasies that come to be realised in fascist movements. The latter, in keeping with Freud's pioneering analyses, are driven by patterns of collective narcissism that persist notwithstanding fascism and Nazism's spectacular defeats. Adorno's analysis remains relevant to our late fascist times. As he writes:

> The economic order, and to a great extent also the economic organization modeled upon it, now as then renders the majority of people dependent upon conditions beyond their control and thus maintains them in a state of political immaturity. If they want to live, then no other avenue remains but to adapt, submit themselves to the given conditions; they must negate precisely that autonomous subjectivity to which the idea of democracy appeals; they can preserve themselves only if they renounce their self. To see through the nexus of deception, they would need to make precisely that painful intellectual effort that the organization of everyday life, and not least of all a culture industry inflated to the point of totality,

prevents. The necessity of such adaptation, of identification with the given, the status quo, with power as such, creates the potential for totalitarianism. This potential is reinforced by the dissatisfaction and the rage that very constraint to adapt produces and reproduces. Because reality does not deliver the autonomy or, ultimately, the potential happiness that the concept of democracy actually promises, people remain indifferent to democracy, if they do not in fact secretly detest it.[33]

Contrary to the perception that his understanding of fascism and anti-Semitism increasingly detached itself from Marxism, Adorno, in his late return to these questions in a 1967 conference on the resurgence of right-wing extremism, discerned the reasons for the continued existence of the social conditions for fascism in the ever-dominant tendency towards the concentration of capital and the consequent waves of *déclassement* and precariousness.[34] Large swathes of surplussed populations came to experience a vacillation of privilege whose libidinal correlate was not just a feeling *of*, but a desire *for*, social catastrophe (and what else would you desire, Adorno suggests, if your economic prospects are dim but you fear real social transformation).

Capitalist abstraction and the spirit of fascism

As I have tried briefly to show, the traces of the problematic of real abstraction originally articulated by Sohn-Rethel can be discerned in Adorno's own efforts to theorise both the actuality of and the potentials for fascism. In the same period, a largely overlooked elaboration of a Marxist theory of the reality of abstraction developed out of a militant and theoretical commitment to anti-fascism, in Norbert Guterman and Henri Lefebvre's 1936 *La conscience mystifiée*.[35]

Guterman and Lefebvre's project, of which *Mystified Consciousness* was to be but a first instalment, was that of forging a science of ideologies in the conjuncture of rising European fascisms and of the (theoretically and politically disoriented) communist and socialist resistance thereto. Guterman and Lefebvre contend that a materialist and proletarian destruction of capitalist fetishism must start with the embodied suspicion that one is 'being dispossessed of one's living existence by abstractions and survivals'.[36] This last formula points to the operation of the real abstractions that fascism cynically feeds upon *and* to the fact that the materiality of ideology is constituted by an often disorderly accumulation and historical sedimentation of seemingly obsolescent forms, beliefs and practices – a theme that chimes with Ernst Bloch's soundings of the dialectic of non-contemporaneity, as well as with Gramsci's conception of 'folklore'.[37] It is in the process of demolishing the mystifications of contemporary 'spiritualism' that Guterman and Lefebvre employ the terminology of 'real abstraction'. As they write: 'The currently declaimed primacy of the spirit means merely the submission to capitalism's myths and weird real abstractions [*étranges abstractions réelles*]. This is direct complicity with the vast lie that results in fascism.'[38] As in Sohn-Rethel's grounding intuition about the identity between the commodity form and the thought form, these real abstractions are to be chased down and back to the simple spatio-temporal praxis that gives rise to them, the banal act of exchange and its corollaries. Though Guterman and Lefebvre's formulation is more poetic than analytical, the resonances with the theses of the author of *Intellectual and Manual Labour* are evident: 'The bloody themes are born of their own accord in our eyes, our mouths, our hands. We must resist the vertigo. The cycle of mystifications is complete, but it is born always and forever from these simple gestures: selling, buying, counting money, reading, thinking.'[39]

According to *La conscience mystifiée*, in modern human beings we encounter

a prodigious heaping up of abstractions, notions, myths ... In effect, our current consciousness is made up of all the experiences and all the interpretations that have appeared in human history, piled up

and tangled without order. Everything can be found here and not
as moments in a totality, but as isolated elements in conflict with
the rest of our consciousness. All the successive formations persist
within us, without being overcome, in a chaos.[40]

'Spirit' – that favourite leitmotiv of conservative revolutionaries and
fascists alike – is the false, superficial, abstract reconciliation of this
incoherent heterogeneity: 'The modern metaphysics of Spirit only
expresses the mystery of capital, the only foundation of all the mys-
teries of this society.'[41] And fascism, we might add more explicitly, is
the reactionary use of sediments in a social atmosphere of capitalist
crisis conditioned by real abstraction and its shearing contradictions.
We may also note here that the 'survivals' of which *Mystified Consciousness* speaks consist of earlier 'layers' of abstraction, in a kind
of geology of (false) consciousness that exerts a shaping pressure
on present praxis.

Anticipating Adorno's subsequent understanding of the potentially fascist nature of coping mechanisms and orienting instruments
under capitalist conditions, Guterman and Lefebvre understand
fascism as instituting a kind of fixity or rigidity to quieten the anxiety
of those living the mental 'vertigo' that arises from the destructive, decadent encounter between 'accumulated abstractions' and
'abstract financial capital' – in a historical phase when all social and
political confidence has collapsed (including trust in what Guterman and Lefebvre call the 'uncertainty of uncertainties: the freedom
of thought, democratic freedom without content'). Accordingly, a
critical (which is to say, a *destructive*) analysis of fascism can't rest
content with tackling reification; it must take aim at the mobile and
morbid nexus between the accumulated abstraction that is Spirit
(what they pointedly term a 'parasite of flesh and action') and the
contemporary abstraction of (parasitic) financial capitalism – with
its train of inflation, speculation, advertising and 'confidence' (or
credit). Writing in the wake of the Great Crash, social abstraction
appears as a kind of unstable 'unreal reality'. But this abstraction

is also 'real' in the sense of being materially embedded: financial capital, Guterman and Lefebvre write,

> never manages to become independent and to separate itself from the capitalist and from production. Abstraction, yes, but one that presupposes an immense material system and apparatus, an abstraction that cannot displace itself above and beyond the rest of the world, opposed as 'concrete', but which intervenes and modifies and concretises itself in acts ... Social relations have been seized by this strange mythology of capital ... Capital sweeps men away in this frightening machinery; it is a phantom with limbs of steel.[42]

Particularly striking here – not least given the affinities between the debates on real abstraction and the 'post-structuralist' fascination with the analogies, isomorphies and short circuits between monetary and signifying economies – is how Guterman and Lefebvre approach the problem of financial capitalism and its violence.[43] They ask: 'What then is finance capital, this master more absolute than ancient despots, which appears as a supreme reality?' Their answer: 'It is nothing but a network of abstract signs, of writing games. But an entire economic and social machine, a whole enormous apparatus of violence, sustains this abstraction ... It is thus at once abstract and terribly concrete.'[44] Marx's insights into how money becomes the only 'real community' in the *Grundrisse* are also echoed when Guterman and Lefebvre write that: 'Social power is anonymous, abstract, faceless [*sans figure*] because it is the power of money.'[45] As with Adorno in *The Authoritarian Personality*, the explanation of the apotropaic appeal of fascist ideology centres on how the psychological burden of systemic opacity is displaced, plugged up, by the fascist solution, at a time when 'social life has never been so obscure'. As they remark:

> This world is strange indeed. Brutal, implacable by its system and its violence. And yet ungraspable, fleeting, abstract. One feels around

oneself brute forces, destinies of a crushing rigidity; and yet the
impression of unreality dominates everything. Where are *beings?*
Who are they? ... What enormous human unreality around and
within us. Because there is no longer anything but an inexpressible
dust of humanity fallen and scattered into multiple and multiform
contradictions. Unhappy consciousness is torn above all by this contradiction: the flight of the real amid the rage to seize it, to possess
it ... The real and illusion – for those who don't escape fascination
in the direction of revolution – are horribly amalgamated. Capital
appears as a reality – or as a mirage. It absorbs reality, dilapidates it,
being nothing itself; but at the same time, it imposes itself brutally
as a reality; it inhibits the consciousness of social and human reality,
and it enables the consciousness of illusion.[46]

The critique of everyday life, for which Lefebvre would come to
be known in the post-war period, draws sustenance from a critique of
real abstraction elicited by the interwar fascist surge. The ideological
fight against fascism cannot be simply, and perhaps not even primarily, a fight against fascist ideology. This is because 'mystification
cannot be the work of ideologues ... they embroider on themes born
in everyday life'. The 'original mystification' takes place in the 'act
of exchange' which is neither barter, speculation or ritual, but the

> constitution of new social relations, the entry onto the stage of
> a complex social process ... By doubling – alienating – itself in
> exchange-value, the object becomes the quantitative fragment of
> an abstraction: homogeneous labour, social, average labour. There
> operates through the fact of exchange (and once this fact is suf-
> ficiently generalised and regularised for there to be a market) a
> general average, a confrontation between all labors that neutralises
> them into an abstract, quantitative, homogeneous substance, the
> only way of making commensurable and comparable qualitative
> labours.[47]

And while Guterman and Lefebvre do not engage in the kind of formal genesis stipulated by Sohn-Rethel, they too contend that any science of ideologies must begin by attending to the act of commodity exchange, thus laying the ground for a conjoined analysis of fascism and fetishism.

Further, as with Sohn-Rethel's concurrent critique of epistemology, this science of ideologies is also an indictment of philosophy as practiced in its time, especially of a metaphysics which, by hypostasising as Spirit or Being the impersonality of capital, and thereby occluding the possibility of its revolutionary destruction, makes its own corrupt contribution to the fascist situation: 'By impersonalising alienation, metaphysicians make it conform more closely to the commodity fetish, more commercial and more manipulable, more acceptable and less painful.'[48] The dual analysis of crisis-ridden capitalist society in terms of *abstraction* and *survivals* comes to invest philosophy itself, delightfully depicted by Guterman and Lefebvre as akin to one of those billionaire's castles built from fragments of cathedrals. By refusing to subject to practical critique its own anachronistic amalgams, spiritualist or metaphysical philosophy stands in the way of a revolution which, understood as the 'realisation of Spirit', involves 'the deployment and ordering of the geologically displaced and piled up strata of capitalist society'. This, as in Bloch, means that no nostalgia for bourgeois Reason is possible: 'This abstraction was already a ruse, a fog in which the germ of the new world wrapped itself up to protect itself. Later, the bourgeoisie would use the same weapon – abstraction – against the new rising class, the proletariat.'[49]

Unlike Sohn-Rethel in his identification of the commodity-form and the thought-form, what Guterman and Lefebvre are after, in sketching out a science of ideology capable of confronting fascism's ideological work – its marshalling of libidinal and utopian energies from multiple pasts and jagged temporalities – is a way of bringing together the real abstractions *and* the accumulated survivals, money *and* myth (or money *as* myth). In other words, and by contrast with the rather linear or monolithic tale of reification and standardisation shared by Adorno and Sohn-Rethel, Guterman and Lefebvre confront us with a different philosophical anthropology, one sensitive to the embodied and embedded role of history and temporality, in all their unevenness, within contemporary ideology. There is no single logic or apparatus of abstraction running smoothly across multiple scales and sectors of capitalist society, and anti-fascist theory as critique of real abstraction cannot operate at the level of the commodity-form and its time alone.

5

Rushing Forward into the Past

Fascism is a cult of the archaic completely fitted out by modern technology. Its degenerate ersatz of myth has been revived in the spectacular context of the most modern means of conditioning and illusion.

Guy Debord, *The Society of the Spectacle*

Fascist times

In the 1930s, Karl Polanyi declared that the *problem* (rather than the movement, program, or regime) of fascism was there at capitalism's inception: a pithy articulation of an understanding of fascism as a potentiality lodged in capital's very marrow. The 'fascist virus' – as the Austro-Hungarian thinker dubbed it – was dormant, but it accompanied capitalism in its longue durée.[1] Reviving the epidemiological simile, Harry Harootunian has recently made the compelling case that we should not treat fascism as a historically remote and finished phenomenon, or alternatively as simply replicable in the present, but should instead grasp it in its historicity, as a mutable response to specific social and political conjunctures:

Like the plague's capacity for mutations, the reappearance of
fascism will not be an exact replica of what existed in the past but
a significant difference reflecting the particular moment. Owing
to its axiomatic relationship to capitalism, the form of fascism, its
destruction of subjective autonomy, remains unchanged, but with
every new reappearance it brings new content in different, historical presents, as Primo Levi observed in the 1970s, when he declared
that every age could expect the return of fascism in new and different materializations.[2]

In a convergent vein, Geoff Eley has argued for a double methodological movement in which the contextualisation of historical
fascisms and their 'dynamics of emergence' are complemented by
a *de-contextualisation* that carefully abstracts from the crises and
conjunctures that gave rise to interwar European fascism and generates a 'portable concept of fascism'. The latter would home in
on fascism's distinctive political pattern, namely 'the coercively
nationalist recourse to political violence and exclusionary authoritarianism under worsening pressures of governing paralysis and
democratic impasse'.[3]

This is an understanding of fascism incompatible with the analogical frame we already criticised in the first chapter. That frame
connects, by way of comparison, a survey of present political phenomena to the past brutalities of European history between 1922 and
1945, with the aim of voicing a warning about a threatened future.
Combining an ideal-typical schema of the steps towards barbarism
with a diagnostic checklist of its symptoms, it is usually countered
by protestations of historical difference, or refutations by disanal-
ogy, rather than by a questioning of the analogical approach as
such. The analogical framing of fascism, which often depends on a
belief in the latter's extraordinariness, tends to obscure capitalism's
congenital potential for violent crisis management as well as its
historical and geographical mutability. As I have already argued,
to recognise capital's constitutive racial and colonial determinations

also means sensitising our historical gaze to the racial fascism that both preceded and conditioned interwar European fascisms. As Eley has also suggested, the contemporary debate over fascism would gain in depth and scope by being cognisant of the multiple origins and forms of fascism:

> Fascism began from East Asia as well as Europe, from Africa as well as the Americas. These fascisms displayed similar political dynamics, ideological outlook, and practices, with convergent political effects. Their partially and unevenly secured access to state power hardly disqualifies them from significance, whether inside their immediate region or in wider transnational political fields. We miss a great deal without this carefully specified global understanding ... The really important point is to dethrone the Nazi and Italian examples – not remotely to diminish their importance, but to see more clearly the broader political space they occupied. The interwar years revealed convergent circumstances of political polarization and societal crisis in many diverse parts of the globe, for which 'fascism' then supplied the shared political language, whether as readily embraced self-description or as the label that opponents bestowed. [4]

But complicating or transcending the analogical frame in our exploration of fascism in the present tense may require more than a reasoned expansion of its geographical scope and historical range. It will demand a consideration not just of fascism's histories but of its temporalities. How we situate fascisms in historical time, and whether we discern them in our present, is also a matter of how fascisms viewed their own time, their own historical moment, and how this vision expressed a specific politics of time. Differences in historical conceptions and political temporalities might offer a privileged prism for thinking through fascism's novel mutations and materialisations in the present.

In approaching the daunting question of fascism and time, it might be useful to distinguish between three levels of abstraction

and analysis. Conscious that the prepositions are hardly unequivocal, I will call these levels the time *for* fascism, the time *in* fascism,
and time *of* fascism.

By the time *for* fascism, I mean to indicate the historical moments
or conjunctures in which fascism appears as a possibility, a con-
tender, a solution. Though disagreements about the fundamental
determinants of fascism's rise continue to pervade theoretical and
historiographic debates, there is broad agreement that the social
temporality of crisis is central to the dynamics of fascism. To ask
about fascism is invariably also to ask about 'fascism-producing
crises'.[5] This time *for* fascism could accordingly be perceived as the
domain of objective, socio-economic analyses. It quickly becomes
apparent, however, that the temporality of crisis – paradigmatically
defined as 'that point in time in which a decision is due but has not
yet been rendered', or as 'a compulsion to judge and act under the
pressure of time' – can never be purged of its intense normative and
subjective charge, as can also be gleaned from Antonio Gramsci's
famous reflections on the interregnum.[6] Nor, indeed, can it be sun-
dered from the fact that 'fascism-producing crises', while anchored
in the vicissitudes of value and the suasion of the state, were also
inextricable from the imminence of social revolution, the aftermath
of military defeat or auguries of national renaissance.[7] The time *for*
fascism, as crisis-time, is also an intrinsically antagonistic time, a
clash of temporalities.

But what if we approach the question of fascism and time from
within, as it were? We could speak here of time for fascists, or better
yet, of time *in* fascism. While none of these levels, as I've just suggested, can be wholly hived off from the others, we can nevertheless
try to circumscribe a 'subjective' dimension of fascist temporality.
What is the place of temporal imaginaries, representations and myths
in fascist ideology? Can we identify something like a phenomenology of temporal experience that would attach to fascist subjectivity?
This is where we can locate the disjunctive synthesis of archaism
and futurity in projects of national-racial rebirth, defined in their

turn by an expansive acceleration of conflict, and by their desire to purge the fascist polity of any obstacles to its self-identity to come.

Mediating the crisis-time *for* fascism and the visions and experience of time *in* fascism is a third level that we could call the time *of* fascism, its objectively subjective temporality, its immanent temporal features. This is the dimension presciently mined by Ernst Bloch in his excavation of fascism's 'non-contemporaneity' – already explored in this book's first chapter – which can be understood as the effort to think together the role of uneven and combined development in fascism's dynamic of emergence with the unevenness that marks classed fantasies and subjectivities in the throes of a fascism-producing crisis.

I will bracket here the question of the time *for* fascism and the comparative symptomatology of ('objective') fascism-producing crises; my focus will be on the interplay between the ('subjective') time *in* fascism and the ('objective-subjective') time *of* fascism. Before moving to a particularly instructive if limited instance of this interplay (the Heidegger case), it may be helpful to synthesise the multiple facets of the relation between fascism and time in a relatively portable manner.

Emerging or intervening in a conjuncture of crisis, also perceived as a political interregnum, a consequence of the unevenness that accompanies capital accumulation and its social forms and formations, fascism mobilises *non-contemporaneity* (of identities, experiences, fantasies, and so on) around a *nostalgic* project of *regeneration, palingenesis, rebirth*, grounded in a view of the present as *decadence, decay, degradation*, consequent upon a *defeat*. Fascism speaks to a *plurality of times* which correlate to the multiplicity of its audiences. In its historical, interwar form, it combined an appropriation and simulation of revolutionary time (for example, Year 1 of the fascist revolution) with an *epochal-millenarian* vision (the Thousand-Year Reich) bolstered by mythologies of *timelessness*. These utopian-apocalyptic perceptions of time screen out fascism's subordination to the capitalist temporalities (of debt, turnover, competition, labour-time) whose contradictions it strives to escape in a flight-forward, an *acceleration*, into a total war economy, or a *deceleration* into a durable form of hyper-reactionary conservatism that only episodically mobilises the chthonic energies of conservative revolution.

Past becoming future: Heidegger and the modernity of fascism

Perhaps the most evident point of identification between fascisms past and proto-fascisms present is distinctly temporal in character. The increasingly widespread pairing of a rhetoric of cataclysmic national decline with hazy promises of rebirth (MAGA, Éric Zemmour's party *Reconquête*, Vox's fetish for the *Reconquista*, and so on), soldered together by the identification of aliens culpable for the general alienation, has led many analysts of the contemporary far right to draw on Roger Griffin's definition of fascism as a 'palingenetic ultranationalism'. There is no doubt that the radical-conservative leitmotivs of decline, decadence, degradation, defeat and destitution loom large in contemporary far-right discourse, closely shadowed by racial narratives of white victimhood and terroristic revanchist fantasies. But are there distinctive temporal markers that might demarcate between ambient authoritarian nostalgias and fascism proper?

In the twentieth century, one of the distinctive features of time *in* fascism, and the one that kept many partisans of tradition at a distance, was the character of its relation to the past, which took as its starting point the radical negativity of the present crisis – the defeat of the nation, the vanishing of tradition, the corruption of the race. If a past was to be reconquered, it was only in a radically revolutionised future. Harootunian has articulated this predicament perspicuously:

> Fascist conceptions of temporality were no more rooted in the
> past, which often was refigured in the present for tactical reasons,

than any other conception of modernity that claimed release from
the burdens of its past. The politics of time built into modernity
concerns the way in which modern societies deal with the question of the past in the present and how they choose to acknowledge
or displace its force. The perceived indeterminacy of an empirical
present and an absent past that is constantly being summoned and
mixing with the new constitutes not so much a resistance to modernity as the principal condition of what it means to become modern.[8]

Writing in the mid-1930s, Henri Lefebvre captured this modernist
penchant of fascism, disavowed by most of its advocates, in the negative dialectic between Nazi ultranationalism and the existence of the
German nation. In the explicit recourse to the mythical register by
Nazi ideologues like Alfred Rosenberg (polemicising against pur-
veyors of an imperialist *Realpolitik*), Lefebvre discerned a belief that
Germany never was but only *becomes* through a sacred and ideal violence, that there is no Nation prior to the bloody work of the political
soldier and the Aryan *condottiere*. Ultimately, this is an avowal that
race itself is a legend, while the nation is 'completely fetishized'.[9]
Nazi ultranationalism must present the nation as not existing *yet* in
order to make the 'national idea' dynamic. The myth of an impos-
sibly distant past everywhere belied by a corrupt present and only
salvageable in a revolutionary future defines a specific temporality
governed by a violent project of purification of self and extermination of the other. The overriding conviction that 'Germany is not; it
is made' warrants the obliteration of any actual lived communities
and differences, sacralising a racial nation-to-come in a 'fleeting, but
terribly demanding, future'.[10] All that is culturally solid melts into
the future of the racial revolution:

> The veritable German community is thus in full dissolution.
> Under the pretext of returning to the deep forces of the soul, of
> the soil, of *Lebensraum*, all the gains of German culture are fought
> and destroyed for the sake of the accidental and the primitive ...

Nationalism can only ground itself ideologically on a myth of origins more or less ably transposed into the future; it is irremediably opposed to national culture.[11]

Peter Osborne's identification of the politics of time that inheres in fascism is helpful here in grasping the latter's *futural* orientation, even at its most apparently nostalgic or archaic. For Osborne, fascism (including National Socialism) is best understood as a variant of the counter-revolutionary ideology that is conservative revolution, which in turn can be captured with Jeffrey Herf's formulation of *reactionary modernism* – with the important caveat that we do not treat this merely as a *contradictio in adjecto* but grasp it instead as

> the modernist temporality of reaction *per se* once the destruction of traditional forms of social authority has gone beyond a certain point … From the standpoint of the temporal structure of its project, fascism is a particularly radical form of conservative revolution. National Socialism was a reactionary avant-garde. It is here that its pertinence to the understanding of modernity as a temporalization of history lies.[12]

In dialogue with Osborne, Griffin has suggested that once we attend to fascism's conservative-revolutionary timecode, 'the core features of its paradoxical temporalities in its various inter-war manifestations fall into place', and we may be better equipped to reflect on the 'hybrid temporality of fascism'.[13]

The purpose of Osborne's delineation of the temporal structure of fascism as a variant of conservative revolution is philosophically to elucidate how Heidegger's rallying to Nazism (and his metapolitical orientation before and after 1933–4) could be understood as the consequence of an underlying politics of time. Osborne rightly points out that, notwithstanding his doctrinal distance from conservative revolutionaries like Carl Schmitt, Ernst Jünger or Oswald Spengler – or the contrasting of his 'spiritual' 'Freiburg National Socialism' to Nazi racial biologism – Heidegger shared with both hardcore Nazis and conservative revolutionaries a temporal-historical horizon, namely 'a diagnosis of the world-historical situation as one of crisis and decline, a nationalist definition of its political shape (conservative revolution as *national* revolution), and a hope for a future grounded in a quite particular revolutionary temporality of renewal'.[14] Osborne makes a compelling case that the temporal structure of Nazism as a political modernism and the affine if irreducible one of Heidegger's *philosophical* modernism can both provide important keys to understanding the politics of reaction, not least in terms of the performative temporal contradiction that marks reactionary modernism as such. This 'bad' modernism is beset by 'the contradiction internal to its temporal structure'. As Osborne argues:

> This structure – the structure of radical reaction within and against modernity – is of necessity contradictory, since one of the things it aims to reverse is the production of the very temporality to which it is itself subject. Radical reaction cannot but reproduce, and thereby performatively affirm, the temporal form of the very thing against which it is pitted (modernity). Hence the necessity for it to misrepresent its temporal structure to itself as some kind of 'recovery' or 'return'.[15]

Conversely, in defining the conditions of possibility of *Dasein*'s historicity in the scholastically martial mode of 'anticipatory resoluteness', Heidegger will turn 'the temporality of modernity against itself, by combining a sense of futurity as the essence of existence (finite transcendence) with the idea of destiny, to produce a radically reactionary point of view'.[16] For Osborne, the latter does not stem from a mere decisionism (which would align Heidegger with Schmitt under the category of 'political existentialists'), but from the specifically temporal concept of repetition advanced in *Being and Time*.[17] It is here that historicity finds itself surreptitiously underwritten and overdetermined by the ideology of national(ist) history:

Heidegger's notion of historicality *narrativizes resoluteness as repetition*: the repetition of the heritage of a people. It thereby provides *Dasein* with a form of historical identification with a definite political meaning. In *authentic* historicality, the possible always (and only) recurs as the possibility of repeating the past ... the present is narrated as crisis and decline (loss of living meaning), while the future appears within the horizon of a 'return to a new beginning' ... It is ... in the mapping of a specific national (and nationalistic) narrative of originary meaning onto the existential structure of resoluteness, via repetition, that the politics of *Being and Time* is to be found.[18]

Fundamental ontology is temporally expressed as nationalist ontology. The nationalization of being and time – along with its martial-sacrificial religion of death – will outlast Heidegger's disillusion with actually existing National Socialism. This is starkly evident, for instance, in the concluding remarks to his lectures from the 1943 Summer Semester on 'The Inception of Occidental Thinking: Heraclitus':

In whatever way the fate of the Occident may be conjoined, the greatest and truest trial of the Germans is yet to come: namely, that trial in which they are tested by the ignorant against their will regarding whether the Germans are in harmony with the truth of beyng, and whether they are strong enough in their readiness for death to save the inceptual ... from the spiritual poverty of the modern world.[19]

A further dimension of what Osborne calls the '*overdetermination of the ontological by the ontical*', of philosophy by a *sui generis* variant of palingenetic ultranationalism, has been compellingly excavated by William Altman in his study of *Being and Time* as a funeral oration for the German fallen of the First World War.[20] Altman takes his cue from a remarkable speech that Heidegger delivered at the twenty-fifth anniversary reunion of his gymnasium in Konstanz, centred on classmates fallen in the war of 1914–18 and suffused with the temporal categories of *Being and Time*. As the ontical marches forward in the figure of the *Frontgemeinschaft* (community of the front) and its comradeship, it is not merely a mythic nation or *Volk* that provides a kind of retroactive 'content' to anticipatory resoluteness, but the very fighting community that Heidegger had not himself joined, the call he had not heeded. The empirical pastness and historiographic factualness of the conflict is what must be broken through, to reconquer historicity from mere history. In his 'funeral oration', Heidegger makes explicit the reactionary politics of repetition and resoluteness that Osborne anatomises. As Heidegger tells his surviving classmates:

> For the Great War comes over us *now* for the *first* time. Our awakening to the two million dead in all those endless graves – which the borders of the Reich and German Austria wear like some mysterious crown – only now begins. The Great War becomes today for us Germans – for us first and foremost among all peoples – the *historical* actuality of our existence for the first time. For history is not that which has been nor even what presents itself but rather what *is to come* and our task with respect to it.[21]

What Hitler's national revolution has 'now' made possible, 'for the *first* time', is an actualisation of the war of 1914–18 *as history*, in view of a *future* task or mission.[22] As Altman astutely notes, the nature of the futurity that repetition makes possible and 'anticipatory resoluteness' actualises is betrayed by Heidegger's talk of 'this gigantic event that we call the First World War'.[23] To speak of a *First World War*, in *1934*, as it comes over 'us' 'now' for the '*first* time' is to enact another fraught move in the politics of time, namely that of transmuting the indefinite, traumatised, anxious but also relieved temporality of the post-war era (*Nachkriegzeit*) into a temporal interregnum between two wars (*Zwischenkriegzeit*) in which one may

answer the call to 'anticipatory [literally *forward-running*] resoluteness', that is, to the future war, the *Second* World War. Having fully
subsumed *Mitsein* (being-with) into a *Front-* and *Volksgemeinschaft*
– into a *generation* produced by 'that binding of oneself to the will'
of the Führer – Heidegger's 1934 reunion speech directly envisages
and calls forth the World War's repetition:

> We who belong to this fully mystical comradeship with our dead
> comrades; our generation is the bridge to spiritual and historical
> victory in the Great War. But only that which has been prepared
> long in advance can build from the ground up for the distant future
> – only what has been decided and which maintains itself perma-
> nently in that decision is able to decide for distant centuries. Mere
> opinions and theories are not effective, programs and organiza-
> tions have no binding power but only this alone: heart to heart and
> shoulder to shoulder![24]

This martial kitsch from an erstwhile shirker, as Altman persuasively argues, nevertheless provides an insight into the temporal
structure of the rather formidable §74 of *Being and Time*. While
a *détournement* or reoccupation of the latter for the purposes of a
non-reactionary politics of time is not unimaginable, it is important
to keep in mind how the marriage of fate and futurity that defines
Dasein's historicity is made possible not just by the temporal structure of conservative revolution, but by the orientation towards the
Great War and its 'repetition' that defined that ideological tendency.[25]
The Reunion Speech does indeed seem to translate (back) the neolo-
gistic contortions of §74 of *Being and Time* into the language of the
Frontgemeinschaft (or Heidegger's pompous approximation thereof).
    It is difficult not to hear the bellicose echoes when Heidegger
writes in *Being and Time* that the

> authentic repetition of a possibility of existence that has been –
> the possibility that Dasein may choose its hero – is existentially

grounded in anticipatory resoluteness; for in resoluteness the choice is first chosen that makes one free for the struggle over what's to come and the fidelity to what can be repeated.[26]

By reading Heidegger's words from 1927 via the effort to repeat 1914 in the speech of 1934, Altman provides an important insight into the temporal structure of Heidegger's conservative revolutionism, his 'private fascism'. Explicating Heidegger's contention that 'if fate constitutes the primordial historicity of Dasein, history has its essential weight in … the authentic occurrence of existence that arises from the *future* of Dasein', Altman writes:

> Only by having explicitly chosen to repeat its *Helden* [heroes] does the 'handing itself down' of the resolute individual become its 'fate'. The temporal paradox central to this passage springs from the fact that the repeatable past becomes the future for 'fateful *Dasein*' … by the explicit decision for *Wiederholung* [repetition]. The decision to embrace the *past* becomes a mission (*Auftrag*) for the *future*, a mission that is simply called 'fate'. To put it simply: past becomes future.[27]

This fated future is perhaps the most sophisticated if cryptic form of that 'nationalisation of eternity'[28] that courses through conservative revolutionary ideology, as was also suggested by Pierre Bourdieu when he observed that:

> The verbal somersault which allows escape from historicism by asserting the essential historicity of the existing, and by inscribing history and temporality within Being, that is, within the ahistorical and the eternal, is the paradigm of all the philosophical strategies of the conservative revolution in philosophical matters. These strategies are always grounded in a radical overcoming which allows everything to be preserved behind the appearance of everything changing.[29]

Difference and repetition in fascism

Repetition, understood as the defining act of a conservative-revolutionary Dasein, undergirds the project for a singularly German 'new beginning' which Heidegger maintained to the war's end. *Future fate*, disclosed by 'freedom-towards-death', is the temporal stamp, the time-myth of his philosophical-political modernism under duress.[30] One of the ideological conditions of possibility for this metapolitical project, as Osborne suggests, is a radical non-reflexivity regarding the temporal structures of the capitalist modernity that conservative revolution and fascism are nominally seeking to transcend, but which shapes them at every step.

Kojin Karatani has suggested that where the first volume of *Capital* mapped the repetition compulsions immanent to the capitalist mode of production, Marx's 1851 *The Eighteenth Brumaire of Louis Bonaparte* offers lasting insights into the repetition compulsions of the nation-state — provided we grasp that historical repetition is a matter of '*form* (structure) and not *event* (content)'.[31] Rather than the mere symptom of the persistence of the *ancien régime*, Bonapartism (and fascism as its twentieth-century avatar) should be perceived as a re-presentation or repetition of absolutist sovereignty — in the understanding that 'the state itself emerges within the crisis of the representative parliament or the capitalist economy. The emperor and the führer are its personifications and are nothing other than the return of the repressed.'[32] The history of liberal democracy remains unintelligible if we don't attend to this structure of repetition. The same goes for fascism, understood as a specific solution to the immanent impasses of political representation. As Karatani observes:

> Representative democracy emerges via the elimination of the absolutist monarch, yet it contains within it a hole that can never be filled. The 'repetition compulsion' within the system of modern democracy is faced with the task of filling that hole in times of crisis

... In thinking of fascism, or of the current political trajectory, it is of decisive importance that all of this emerges only by way of representation in a general election.[33]

Straddling both the time *in* and *of* fascism – to employ the distinctions sketched above – the project of breaking through into the past, of *making* the primal (racial) nation exist *for the first time*, is shaped by its contradictory relationship to capital's temporality of creative destruction, of the *now* and the *new*. But we should also be attentive to how the revival of a violent desire to return, the repetition of a politics of repetition, is rendered possible at the level of both the capitalist economy and (its) nation-state.[34] As Harootunian has suggested, it is

the relationship to the commodity form that is missing in most accounts of fascism and that offers a plausible explanation for its capacity to return punctually, as well as its own suppression of history for the mystery of myth and origin (like the nation-form itself) and its predilection for repetition.[35]

If fascism can be captured as the organised desire for a 'capitalism without capitalism', then it is crucially a capitalism that disavows capitalist temporality, covering over the time of the commodity with that of spiritual revolution, the time of turnover with that of racial-national rebirth.[36] And, we could add, this relationship, and its temporal determinants, is also foreclosed from conservative revolutionary and fascist thought themselves, which evade the time of capital, surreptitiously congealing it into mythical and diabolically impersonal agents like the Machine or Technology, or racialised and conspiratorial fantasies of a nomadic, 'globalist', calculating rationality.[37] We could accordingly connect, via the problem of repetition, the time *in* fascism (the figure of a forward-flight into the archaic, 'future fate' as the stamp of palingenetic ultranationalism) with the time *for* fascism, understood in terms of 'the status of capitalist accumulation and its propensity for producing crises everywhere in the form of a structurally determined unevenness, rather than merely attesting to the signs of arrest and delay', and more specifically, with an eye on the present, of 'the repetition driving liberalism, which, in its new neoliberal avatar, is even more determined to overcome the "defects" of incompleteness by resorting to ever-greater measures to satisfy the appetite of a self-regulating market, which promotes unevenness'.[38] Mediating fascist visions and fascism-producing crises is that objective-subjective level which I called the time of fascism. This is the domain of the social and psychic life of unevenness that Harootunian explores, and it is here that fascism's temporal manipulations have exercised their greatest force and fascination – rather than in the reactionary philosophical-political (and aesthetic) modernisms that sought, and failed, to lead the leaders as the latter led the masses.

For if fascism is indeed a 'scavenger' ideology, scooping up 'scraps of Romanticism, liberalism, the new technology, and even socialism', it also reclaimed and recombined their temporal imaginaries and styles, as well as those stemming from contiguous or precursor ideological positions (radical nationalism, traditionalism, anti-Semitism, racial imperialism and so on).[39] Fascism was (and remains) able to weaponise a kind of structured incoherence in its political and temporal imaginaries, modulating them to enlist and energise different class fractions, thereby capturing, diverting and corrupting popular aspirations. In 1921, Mussolini himself had brashly advertised fascism's 'super-relativism', in keeping with the modern supremacy, including and especially in the sciences, of relativity over objectivism. His floridly bombastic declaration demonstrates there is nothing particularly 'postmodern' about mixing authoritarian violence with eclecticism and irony (unless we wish to tag fascism itself as postmodern):

For those who boast of always being the same as themselves, nothing is more relativistic than the fascist mentality and fascist action. If relativism and universal movementism (*mobilismo*) are equivalent, we fascists, who have always manifested our unscrupulous arrogance (*strafottenza*) towards the nominalisms to which the sanctimonious bigots of other parties nail themselves, like bats to rafters; we, who've had the courage of breaking into smithereens all the traditional political categories and calling ourselves, depending on the moment, aristocrats and democrats, revolutionaries and reactionaries, proletarian and anti-proletarian, pacifists and anti-pacifists, we are really the relativists *par excellence* and our action resonates directly with the most current movements of the European spirit.[40]

We can thus speak of fascism's temporal pluralism and relativism, where different ritualised or symbolised temporal markers are broadcast to distinct audiences across fascism's multiple publics. As the returns of capitalist crisis elicit the reactionary politics of repetition, they also dredge up a not necessarily coherent or cohesive multiplicity of experiences and fantasies of a lost past of order and hierarchy, as imaginary resolutions of the crisis accompany political moves to secure it for the forces of capital. The challenge for any fascist resolution of crisis is to carry out the articulations or disjunctive syntheses that allow it to mediate the time of resentment or revanchism (the time of identity, and indeed of race) with the time of accumulation (the time of value), while drawing on a disorderly archive of sedimented temporal imaginaries and experiences.

As the Brazilian literary critic Roberto Schwarz noted in a recent interview on 'neo-backwardness' in Bolsonaro's Brazil, the problem that we are once again confronting is that of 'the combination, at moments of crisis, of the modern and the oldest of the old', the re-emergence of a 'retrogressive-modernizing solution ... that allowed capitalism to advance, while society continued to indulge in the same old inequalities' precisely by mobilising seemingly anachronistic temporal imaginaries.[41] In seeking to understand fascism's temporalities, we cannot simply dwell on its modernism under duress but must attend to the way in which social life is criss-crossed by plural temporalities. The class structure of modern society is shadowed by multiple cultural and historical times that do not exist synchronously, though they come to be articulated or 'formally subsumed' under the time of capital. As we encountered in our discussion of Bloch's theory of fascist temporality in this book's first chapter, that non-synchronicity is itself historically and materially inflected, and today's amalgams of archaism and futurism are not those of the 1930s. But Bloch's insights can still resonate. His aim was to counter fascism as a swindle of fulfilment while taking seriously the urges for social and human plenitude it seized upon and diverted for the purposes of domination. Among fascism's scavenged treasures was also utopia. And fascist scavenging was to be countered by communist salvage.

Counter-revolution without revolution

While there's no shortage of nostalgia for a fascist modernity willing to pastiche reactionary modernisms and archaic futurisms in novel discursive and communicative ecologies, the time *of* fascism's current incarnations is, arguably, not a revolutionary time but one of both lateness and incipience – as we explored in our discussion of racial fascism. This temporality can be understood in terms of the gathering cohesion of disparate fascist potentials under crisis conditions, but also in relation to the shapes taken by reaction in non-revolutionary times. Just as the lens of non-contemporaneity needs to be adjusted to the different modalities of unevenness in our present, so does that of incipience, which is repeated here with a difference.

What, we may wonder, is late fascism trying to prevent? Here is where the superstructure sometimes seems to overwhelm the base, as though forces and fantasies once functional to the reproduction of a dominant class and racial order had now attained a kind of autonomy.[42] No imminent *political* threat to the reproduction of capitalism is on the horizon, so that contemporary fascist trends manifest the strange spectacle of what, in a variation on Angela Y. Davis and Herbert Marcuse's 1970s analyses of the new faces of fascism, we could call a *preventive counter-reform* — as evidenced by panics over 'critical race theory', 'gender ideology', and the like.[43]

On a more optimistic note, that progressive or liberal reforms may appear to racists and reactionaries as signs of a communist dystopia that is almost already here could also be interpreted as the distorted recognition of utopian traces that demand to be blasted out of the continuum of reformism. An ideal for the left might be to become what its enemies think it already is, namely a strategically ingenious and systematic endeavour to undermine white, Western, Christian, capitalist, patriarchal civilisation across all institutions of society.

To the extent that preventive counter-reform also seeks to capture a diffuse malaise bodied forth by the pathologies of late capitalism,[44] it will appear in the guise of proto-fascism, that

> shifting strategy of class alliances whereby an initially strong populist and anticapitalist impulse is gradually readapted to the ideological habits of a petty bourgeoisie, which can itself be displaced when, with the consolidation of a fascist state, effective power passes back into the hands of big business.[45]

This proto-fascism, the kind flaunted by reactionary modernists like Wyndham Lewis, defined itself against Marxism, the 'taboo position' that it was compelled both to repel and displace, while viewing itself 'as the implacable critique of the various middle class ideologies and of the parliamentary system in which they find representation'.[46]

Orbiting around the fantastical foci of 'cultural Marxism' and related leftist conspiracies, on the one hand, and 'globalism' (or 'metropolitan elites'), on the other, our own late proto-fascism also operates in the ambiguous space opened up by the structural inconsistency between its anti-systemic postures and its anti-anti-systemic animus (anti-communism without communism is one of the more tragicomic symptoms of fascism's 'lateness'). This is the space where 'a critique of capitalism can be displaced and inflected in the direction of classical petty-bourgeois ideology', characterised by its regressive fantasies of social harmony, moral hierarchies, and the hegemony of property without financialised capital's inscrutable abstractions and destabilising dynamics.[47]

If interwar fascism was 'a new movement in a hurry', both desperately seeking tradition and obsessed with 'the speed of time', its current epigones are marked by a far less unequivocal rhythm and momentum.[48] While not devoid of their own shop-worn epochal or conspiratorial time-myths ('the Fourth Turning', 'the Great Replacement', 'the Great Reset'), they germinate in the context of a more distended crisis. Even if we don't set our present predicament in the context of a long downturn beginning in the 1970s, it is worth noting that the time elapsed between the 2007–8 credit crunch and today matches the full duration of German fascism. Albeit endowed with a vicious 'accelerationist' fringe, acting out the impotent belief that spectacular carnage might trigger mass upheavals, the time *of* contemporary fascisation is generally far slacker, more ambivalent, more conservative than revolutionary in its fantasies. It is transfixed by the mirage of 'regeneration with security' and the return not so much to the archaic future of the sublime nation and race to-come but to the remaindered modernity of a post-war compact, one of whose conditions of possibility, ironically, was fascism's defeat.

6

Ideas without Words

Statistically, myth is on the right. There, it is essential; well-fed, sleek, expansive, garrulous, it invents itself ceaselessly … The oppressed *makes* the world, he has only an active, transitive (political) language; the oppressor conserves it, his language is plenary, intransitive, gestural, theatrical: it is Myth. The language of the former aims at transforming, of the latter at eternalizing.

— Roland Barthes, *Mythologies*

Mapping right-wing culture

How and why is the current ecology of reaction primarily nourished by conflicts, nay 'wars', that are framed as *cultural* – even when, as in the leitmotiv of a forgotten white working class, the superstructure is nothing but a fever dream of the base? In this chapter, I want to approach these questions by taking some distance from the framing of these problems in terms of social media moral panics and their false immediacies, drawing instead on a little-known but extremely fecund source for thinking the fates and futures of the radical right, namely the 1979 book *Cultura di destra* (Right-Wing Culture) by the Italian Germanist and mythologist Furio Jesi (1941–1980).

Jesi's unique and protean work is only beginning to make inroads into Anglophone debates.[1] Having begun his extremely precocious scholarly career in his teens as an Egyptologist and archaeologist, after dropping out of high school (his first book on tales and legends of ancient Rome, co-authored with his mother, was published when he was fifteen, his treatise on Egyptian pottery at seventeen), Jesi produced uniquely perceptive monograph studies of Rousseau, Brecht, Bachofen, Kierkegaard, as well as dozens of dense, playful and iconoclastic essays on topics ranging from the work of his erstwhile mentor, the Hungarian mythologist Karl Kerényi, to the writings of Elias Canetti and Ezra Pound. *Cultura di destra* was published a year before Jesi's death from an accidental gas-leak in his home, and in the midst of an extremely violent season – both physically and discursively – in Italian politics, which would culminate, a month and a half after Jesi's death, in the bombing of the train station in Bologna, a massacre imputed to far right terrorists, some of whom found inspiration in texts, such as those of Julius Evola or Giorgio Freda, touched upon in *Cultura*.[2]

Not least among the reasons for turning to Jesi's book four decades on, in this morbid conjuncture, has to do with the recombinant lives of an esoteric revolutionary-conservative right in our metastasising media spheres. Jesi's observation about the logorrheic habits of reactionary keepers of secret and elite knowledge is still germane: 'Most of the sages of modern esoterism … have spent their life proclaiming that their wisdom was inaccessible and incommunicable by words, while at the same time being the most prolific of polygraphs.' Today we are not just witnessing the recovery and republishing of the likes of Evola, Oswald Spengler, Ernst von Salomon and others, but the revival of right-wing culture more broadly, understood, as Jesi declared in a 1979 interview with the Italian weekly *L'Espresso*, as that 'culture in which it is declared that there are values beyond debate, indicated by capitalised words, above all Tradition and Culture but also' – underscoring the right-wing form of much self-described leftist culture – 'Justice, Freedom, Revolution. A culture, in other words, made up of authority, mythological security about the norms of knowing, teaching, commanding, and obeying.' This culture is one in which 'the past becomes a kind of processed mush [*pappa omogeneizzata*, baby food] that can be modelled and readied in the most useful way possible'.[3]

Jesi captured the production, hypostasis and circulation of these powerfully vacant, capitalised signifiers in a formula drawn from Spengler's last book, *Jahre der Entscheidung* (The Hour of Decision), written before but published shortly after Hitler's rise to power. In the preface to that book – which Jesi otherwise passes over but which we'll return to below – Spengler wrote: 'That which we have in our blood by inheritance – namely wordless ideas – is the only thing that gives permanence to our future.'[4] Jesi contends that the men of culture of the radical and fascist right

> had at their disposal a genuine literary language suited to 'ideas without words'. This was not a language they had invented. It was a language created in the bosom of bourgeois culture, matured in the course of the relations with the past which that culture had configured, and ready for use.[5]

Jesi's thesis is encapsulated in the following formulation:

> The language of ideas without words is dominant in what today is printed and said, and its printed and spoken acceptations – in which recur those words which have been spiritualised enough so that they can serve as vehicles for ideas that require non-words – can also be found in the culture of those who do not want to be on the right, that is to say of those who should resort to words that are 'material' enough to be the vehicle of ideas that demand words. This stems from the fact that the greatest part of our cultural heritage [*patrimonio*], even of those who by no means want to be on the right, is a cultural residue of the right.[6]

Notwithstanding its wallowing in hollow clichés and vapid tokens of belonging, the culture of the right is for Jesi, at this linguistic level, *formally esoteric*, since it relies on a 'morphological and syntactical skeleton of ideas, which entertain precarious, temporary and approximative relationships with words'.[7] The continuity that underlies right-wing culture, and its suffusion through much of the *soi-disant* left, is not, according to Jesi, a continuity of words but is dictated by

> the choice of a language of *ideas without words*, which presumes that one can truly speak – meaning speak and at the same time cloak in the secret sphere of the symbol – while doing without words, or better not worrying overmuch about symbols as modest as words, unless they are watchwords, slogans. Whence the nonchalance in the use of stereotypes, clichés, recurrent formulae; it is not just a matter of cultural impoverishment, of a vocabulary objectively limited by dint of ignorance: the language which is used is, above all, that of *ideas without words* and it can rest content with few terms or syntagms: what matters is the closed circulation of the 'secret' – myths and rituals – which the speaker shares with the listeners, and which all the participants in the assembly or the collective have in common.[8]

The religion of death

A year prior to the publication of *Cultura*, Jesi had published a corrected edition of Evola's 1957 translation of Spengler's *Decline of the West*, on which he had collaborated with colleagues at the University of Palermo (his first academic posting, after having worked mainly in publishing). His introduction, excised from later editions, was harshly criticised by those who mistakenly saw it as a kind of Lukácsian polemic, in the mode of the Hungarian philosopher's *The Destruction of Reason*, instead of as the brilliant and politically charged philological investigation that it is. In it, Jesi explored the

nexus of poetics and mythology in early twentieth-century Munich
– where Spengler wrote *Decline* and lived from 1911 to his death in
1936 – and its shaping impact on the German thinker's historical-
philosophical attention to the 'rhythms of the time of the secret,
marked by the seasons of myth'.[9] Jesi identified in the debates
around the work of the jurist, mythologist and author of *Mother
Right*, Johann Jakob Bachofen, some of the sources of Spengler's
appropriation of a key theme in the poetics of 'secret Germany' and
in the culture of the right more broadly, namely the *religio mortis*,
the religion of death.[10]

As Jesi wrote: 'Spengler's Bachofen was the connoisseur of funerary symbols of a religion of death to which there belonged heroes,
but defeated heroes ... a power that is in continual interaction with
defeat.'[11] Jesi argued that the notion of 'cultural circles' (*Kulturkre-
ise*) and

> the seasons of the para-biological becoming of cultures are, in
> Spengler, schemas for an appreciation of history which has at its
> centre the experience of death and defeat. Culture becomes aware
> of itself in the instant in which it self-destructs, or in which it is
> destroyed by a force which contains in itself the germ of its own
> extinction.[12]

Spengler's pessimism 'bases its oracular eloquence and its epistemology of clairvoyance on ambitions of pure prophecy in the ambit of a
religio mortis'.[13] In this ideological horizon, defeat is transfigured into
the sacrament of a political religion of death. Nowhere is the symbology of defeat more emphatically evident than in the closing lines of
the 1931 *Man and Technics*, where, after prophesying the inevitable
overcoming of 'Faustian' white civilisation by the coloured world
revolution, Spengler declaims:

> We are born into this time and must bravely follow the path to
> the destined end. There is no other way. Our duty is to hold on

to the lost position, without hope, without rescue, like that Roman soldier whose bones were found in front of a door in Pompeii, who, during the eruption of Vesuvius, died at his post because they forgot to relieve him. That is greatness. That is what it means to be a thoroughbred. The honourable end is the one thing that can not be taken from a man.[14]

The theme of a literary, mythological and political 'religion of death' is at the heart of Jesi's anatomy of the culture of the right. It had already occupied Jesi's attention in his *Secret Germany* and his many writings on Thomas Mann, and it was similarly central to his critical engagement with the poet and novelist Cesare Pavese, who in his capacity as co-editor, with the philosopher and ethnologist Ernesto De Martino, of Einaudi's famous *Collana viola* (the 'Collection of Religious, Ethnological and Psychological Studies'), commissioned and oversaw translations of Kerényi, Eliade, Frobenius, Jung, Lévy-Bruhl and others, which would have an outsize effect on critical discussions of mythology in the Italian post-war era. Long before the publication of pages from his secret wartime notebooks revealed a Pavese open to the fascination of fascist motifs, Jesi had discerned in the Piedmontese writer – whose rallying to the Italian Communist Party in 1945 was not least of the PCI's cultural coups – the effect of a *religio mortis* nourished by the German poetry and literature of the early twentieth century.[15] Indeed, where Pavese was wont to present his ethnological influences as an enlightened check on the darker powers of myth, Jesi saw in them the imprint of that literary manipulation of mythological materials that marked the poetic and intellectual galaxy of 'secret Germany'. As Jesi programmatically declared in his 1964 essay on 'Pavese, Myth and the Science of Myth':

Secret Germany: it doesn't seem rash to define it as that religion of death that was doubly 'secret', both because it proceeds from the innermost 'secret' of poets, and because it is perennially masked beneath the defences of consciousness, save, perhaps, in Rilke. 'Public', rather than 'secret' Germany, demonstrated with Nazi ideology its effort to try and appropriate that secret current and to turn it into a social and popular reality, stripping its status as the property of the undoubtedly 'aristocratic' circles in which it had hitherto lived. The repugnance of Kerényi and Mann, faced with the demonstrations of the Nazi youth, testifies to a hostility that developed between the 'public' and the 'secret' Germany, when the former wanted to take possession of the latter.[16]

Jesi was critical of the disguises (*mascherature*) that the religion of death received at the hands of figures like Mann and Kerényi, while never doubting the genuineness of their anti-fascism. Likewise, he saw in Pavese's effort to write and live tragically, and in his eventual suicide, a particular inflection of the *religio mortis*, grounded in the irrevocable loss of *lived, collective* myth, now deconsecrated and reduced to personal mythologies of childhood, leading to an inability to save historical time through the ritual technique of the ancient festival – where the latter, *la festa*, is understood as the carnal, embodied forum for the experience of myth. Incapable of the 'Faustian compromises' and felicitous mystifications that allowed Mann to create rich mythological tapestries in works like *Joseph and His Brothers*, Pavese's novels could only portray faded afterimages of a now impossible festival, simulacra of initiation, in a world where emblematic words were now devoid of magico-religious efficacy, while his own personal and poetic trajectory had as its 'dynamic norm ... the substitution of the myth of the festival with the myth of sacrifice'.[17] Pavese's communism too, dominated by the themes of duty, sacrifice and guilt (not least at his own lack of wartime commitment, his evasion of the Resistance) could also be seen as shadowed by such a *religio mortis*.

But where Pavese sought to produce a poetics that was the 'moral theorisation of the need to act and live even if the city is deconsecrated and the sacred treasure of the countryside are no longer accessible', one in which the link of *ethos* and *mythos* took the form of a human sacrifice (figural and personal) at the end of a profane festival, the right-wing culture anatomised in Jesi's 1979 book would entertain a far less tragic and far more instrumental relation to the secret if hollow heart of the mythological machine.[18]

Winning by dying

The first of the two essays that compose *Cultura di destra*, 'Right-Wing Culture and the Culture of Death', is a signal example of the 'knowledge by composition' that defined Jesi's philological art. Beginning with an appreciation of the consumption of 'spiritual luxury' evident in the manipulation of the 'eternal and metamorphic values' of an undefined past in a Jugendstil design magazine, Jesi ranges across Frobenius's disquisitions on German science, the racial underpinnings of primitivism, funerary symbolism, the figure of Jack the Ripper in the writings of Frank Wedekind and Aleister Crowley, and E. T. A. Hoffmann's novella *Der Vampir* read as an allegorical-prophetic text about German Nazism. He also comments on the loss of centre that characterises the monumental scenography and architecture of Nazism, understood as '*defensive* rituals of "foundation"', and the panicked Judeophobia at the core of the Nazi regime, including the occult and ethnological investigations of Himmler's *Ahnenerbe* – the SS's research institute for the study of 'ancestral heritage', in which Jesi glimpsed 'the mythology of killing and being killed as the procedure of acceleration and advent of the foundation of a new kingdom, a new law, a new man'. While registering in Nazism the traits of bourgeois instrumentality and capitalist domination, Jesi does not shy away from taking seriously the idea of a Nazi esotericism, stemming from the exterminatory-sacrificial core of a right-wing *religio mortis*. Viewed from this perspective, the 'religion and mythology of death are the defensive and tragic – but not despairing – reaction of those who, like the protagonists of Nazi power and ritualism, feel abandoned,

beset, "poisoned" by adversaries who in their turn proclaim themselves as elect'.[19]

But Jesi's most incisive words on the *religio mortis* of the right are
drawn not from Nazism or Italian Fascism – with its petty bourgeois
coldness and cynicism vis-à-vis mythology and its 'superficial death-
mysticism' hiding an 'interested optimistic and vitalist cynicism'
– but from the Spanish Falange and the Romanian Iron Guard.[20]
It is with reference to the latter that Jesi tackles the nexus of myth,
death and politics in the writing of Mircea Eliade – whose book *Yoga*
Jesi had edited and who was shaken by what he, Eliade, perceived
as a 'perfidious attack' by the young Italian scholar.[21] Compared
to the poverty of the Francoist call '*Abajo la inteligencia! Viva la
muerte!*' (down with intelligence, long live death) shouted by the
general José Millán-Astray against Miguel de Unamuno in the aula
magna of the University of Salamanca in 1936, the Romanian Iron
Guard and its intellectual auxiliaries boasted a much headier brew
that mixed together Orthodox Christianity, non-Christian esotericism, references to the 'Orphism' of ancient Thrace, the racist and
telluric anthropology of authentic Romanian man, anti-Semitism
and anti-Westernism.

But Jesi focuses especially on the funereal eroticism of Eliade's
version of a Romanian ballad about Master Manole, the tale of a
mason compelled to immure his own wife to complete his construction. Jesi notes Eliade's then recently revealed fascist past, his
writings on the redemption of the ethnic stock in the 'legionnaire
revolution' of the Iron Guard, his mourning for its leader Corneliu
Zelea Codreanu, his work as cultural attaché in Lisbon for the same
government that deported thousands of Jews – but also Eliade's
'discovery of non-European man and his spiritual universe', which
for Jesi was no antidote to racial fascism. But Jesi's chief evidence
lies in that exquisitely sacrificial logic of *winning by dying* (*vincere
morendo*), which he discerns at the core of right-wing culture and
which makes the legend of the mason Manole into the 'veritable *hieros
logos* [holy word] of that religion of death'. This is the 'ideology'

common to multiple myths of sacrifice which Eliade himself encapsulated as follows:

> To last, a construction (house, technical accomplishment, but also a spiritual undertaking) must be animated, that is, must receive both life and a soul. The 'transference' of the soul is possible only by means of a sacrifice; in other words, by a violent death. We may even say that the victim continues its existence after death, no longer in its physical body but in the new body – the construction – which it has 'animated' by its immolation; we may even speak of an 'architectonic body' substituted for a body of flesh. The ritual transference of life by means of a sacrifice is not confined to constructions (temples, cities, bridges, houses) and utilitarian objects: human victims are also immolated to assure the success of an undertaking, or even the historical longevity of a spiritual enterprise.[22]

Developing, in an original and unsettling direction, Horkheimer and Adorno's insights into the mimetic character of anti-Semitism, Jesi proceeds to identify the 'secret message' of Eliade's doctrine – the notion that myths and religions are product of God's withdrawal from this world – as ultimately grounded in an appropriation of Jewish Kabbalistic doctrine. The latter, in turn, found its most intense expression in the messianic heresies of Sabbatai Zevi and Jakob Frank, where just as 'God "withdraws" so that creation may take place, the Messiah infringes the law so that the epiphany of the new law may come'.[23] Jesi even identifies a paradoxical coincidence between the mystical self-portraits of the persecutors and the persecuted, between the theme of winning by dying in the sacrificial right and the Jewish messianic nexus of guilt and transgression. Here lies 'the tragicness of the condition [of Zevi, the holy sinner]: the law that he transgressed had to be transgressed for the new law of the new kingdom'.[24] In the wake of God's self-exile, and through the perverse and surreptitious appropriation of this esoteric Jewish tradition, there emerges in Eliade's speculations on the religions of sacrifice a figure of the fascist martyr, who chooses to embrace guilt in order to accelerate the coming of the new world.

Exoteric and esoteric fascisms

The second essay in *Cultura di destra*, 'The Language of Ideas without Words', reprises the Spenglerian motif of wordless ideas to explore the relation between a sacred esoteric fascism and a profane exoteric one, in the understanding that these do not overlap with the then-common distinction in Italy between a respectable, 'besuited' fascism and a violent, plebeian one. Here Jesi ranges widely across the productions of the radical right – from obsequious studies of the SS's European volunteers and their ties to the occult tradition of templars and mages to Julius Evola's preface to the *Protocols of the Elders of Zion*, passing through the eroticisation of Mussolini in fascist novels of the *ventennio*. Reprising the theme of the useless task and the virile apology of defeat, while referencing neo-fascist bombings and murders, Jesi remarked: 'We can by no means exclude this: that at least some of the terrorist acts of the last few years were projected as useless tasks by the instructors and didacts of the Tradition, who led the neophytes to believe that they were in themselves *useful* tasks for them.'[25]

The constellation in which Jesi places the 1970s nexus between Tradition and terror demonstrates a desire to chart the indefinite domain of wordless ideas – spanning the sacred and the profane, the esoteric and the exoteric – into regions that force us to relinquish the comforts that would derive from treating right-wing culture as the sole monopoly of avowed fascists or Nazis. Jesi's desecrating montage of several symptomatic specimens of the language of ideas without words places Evola – once hailed by the neo-fascist politician Giorgio Almirante as 'our Marcuse' – in contiguity with a meticulous analysis of two speeches commemorating the national poet Giosuè Carducci delivered by Jesi's maternal grandfather, Percy Chirone.[26] This is followed by a brilliantly caustic philology of a salient product of twentieth-century Italian culture industry, Liala, a bestselling author of romantic feuilleton novels (and associate of poet and fascist precursor Gabriele D'Annunzio), and a caustic segue into a journalistic profile of Ferrari CEO and aristocrat Luca Cordero di Montezemolo. What brings such seemingly heterogeneous figures together? A certain linguistic use of the past that orbits around signifiers of spiritual and material 'luxury' that are both connoted as elite and designed for general consumption. This is a language pervaded by acts of devotion to the fetish of spiritualised property, including the typically fascist spiritualisation of industry itself – an aestheticisation of the economy that doggedly disavows the impersonality and automatism of capital. But it also revolves around precious symbols, the luxury fetishes of the right: 'The Graal, symbolic flowers, the zodiac, the swastika, the cave, the labyrinth, the rainbow, etc'.[27]

While cutting across disparate genres (metapolitical tracts for initiates, eulogies, mass-market literature) and addressing distinctive audiences (adepts of tradition, patriots or freemasons, petty bourgeois housewives), all the texts surveyed by Jesi register the 'ideological need to flatten the differences that history posits in the past and to manipulate a compact, uniform and substantially undifferentiated value' – a value that in the speeches of Jesi's grandfather circulates through such vapid and proto-fascistic formulae as 'a masculine visage', 'virile pride' and 'fateful historical moments'.[28] Value here stands for military valour as well as the value of 'valuable stuff'. The language of the right operates like a luxury good, but so does its undifferentiated, sacralised, empty image of the good, desirable death. It is the dedifferentiation of the past as value that allows it to circulate so easily in the present. This is a language that draws on a whole inherited cultural apparatus which is 'technicized' and 'transformed into a culture-fetish, sacral and *exoteric*.[29] Cultural elements are as it were homogenised: in this mush, this baby food, which is declared to be precious but also digestible by the passably educated classes, there are no longer real contrasts, edges, thorns, or asperities.'[30]

It is an idiom of lyrical commonplaces presented as a 'model of clarity', understandable by all. It chimes with the intimate, affective appeal of the cliché-ridden vapidities of Liala's romances, which operate with a language that is efficacious to the extent that it is not rationally comprehensible but is instead emotionally grasped:

> If it really were comprehensible, it would not have that magical effi-cacy, it would make one think, and thus toil, and it would compel one to exercise one's capacity to understand what is happening. Liala's language is not *understood* by all her readers; but it is for all her readers a fetish that serves to give pleasure, and especially the pleasure stemming from the reduction of the fatigue that comes from thinking.[31]

The language of the right declares clarity but channels the obscure, camouflages its repugnance for history under the worship of a glori-ously hollow past, while 'its truly corpselike immobilism feigns to be a perennial living force'.[32]

Gratuitous brutality

In tacit dialogue, no doubt, with Walter Benjamin's critique of the fascist aestheticisation of politics, the final section of Jesi's study of the culture of the right undertakes a parallel reading of two towering para-fascist writers, Gabriele D'Annunzio and Luigi Pirandello. Its focal point is the theme, already rehearsed in the treatment of neo-fascist culture, of the 'brutality of the useless gesture'. Jesi presents D'Annunzio, by contrast with his legions of followers, as a somewhat liminal, even tragic figure who, while a master at the technicisation of mythological materials, seems to realise, despite himself, that the past of myth could not be manipulated at will. His political histri-onics notwithstanding, 'beyond the undifferentiated past which he continuously manipulated, [D'Annunzio] came up against a past composed of distinctly differentiated hypostases, a lost past.'[33] This tonality of irretrievable loss, of metaphysical and metahistorical defeat – already noted in Jesi's introduction to Spengler and in the neofascist esotericism of Evola and his epigones – characterises the useless task, the right-wing marriage of pessimism and activism. This is a posture vouchsafed by reference to a homogenised past and crystallised as a practice of brutality. As Jesi comments:

> All the spiritual luxury of right-wing culture corresponds to a brutality of public and private, social and familial behaviour. This does not appear in the least gratuitous to its apologists, so long as the latter are satisfied with the undifferentiated past with which they fabricate fetishes of virility, heroic strength, sacrifice unto death, discipline, hierarchy, fatherland and family to defend as their iron-clad possessions, and as long as they believe that the mush they manipulate truly is life's eternal present (the true atemporal past, *ergo* the true present).[34]

This is the framework, or better the *style*, that is common, for instance, to D'Annunzio and the 'sacred and esoteric fascism' that orbits around Evola. It is the style of winning by dying, of homicidal self-immolation, of a morbid, sacrificial 'heroism' – which is of course, as Jesi notes, eminently manipulable for profoundly exoteric purposes, as testified to by the role played by that 'sacred right' in the Italian deep state's 'strategy of tension'. Useless tasks for useful idiots. But commonalities are not homogeneities; Jesi's philological capacity to discriminate among modalities of right-wing culture, language and poetics is among his greatest lessons for us – as we see for instance in his clinical differentiation between the brutalising aesthetics of the useless task in D'Annunzio and Pirandello. While D'Annunzio's is a didactic mystification, tinged with tragedy and oriented toward future cosmic revelations, 'Pirandello's is a useless brutality without mystification, for it is a brutality made useless, nihilistic, and profoundly exoteric by the loss of any collective past, and therefore also of any future'.[35] More proof, if proof were needed, that fascistic violence is not correlated with either the sacred or the profane, and that the *religio mortis* can have its aesthetic-political afterlives even after religion's demise.

Fear of a Black planet

While he wrote in a radically different media ecology than our own, I don't think it is necessary to belabour why Jesi's reflections on the nexus between the aesthetics of the useless task, *religio mortis* and the language of ideas without words may provide tools with which to think against our own present – that grotesque genre which is the prolix and self-pitying plagiarised manifesto of the lone male racist mass shooter might be testimony enough.[36] But I would like to conclude this chapter in a somewhat different vein, by tarrying some more with Spengler's wordless ideas.

Jesi does not in fact say much about the book from which that formulation was taken. Let me turn then to an anonymous review of the original edition of *The Hour of Decision*, published in *Il Popolo d'Italia* in December 1933. The reviewer summarises the book's thesis, quite faithfully, as follows:

> That the world is threatened by two revolutions: one white and one coloured. The white revolution is the 'social' one and it is the catastrophic result of the collapse of civilization in the eighteenth century and the advent of the reign of the masses, especially those that cluster – soulless and faceless – in the big cities, a process which took place in the nineteenth century, under the sign of liberalism, democracy, universal suffrage, and what is globally known as demagogy. The other revolution is that of the peoples of colour, who, being more prolific than the peoples of the white race, will eventually overwhelm it. Therefore, for us, Europeans of the twentieth century, the question arises: What to do? Spengler does not answer this agonizing question very clearly.

The reviewer was Benito Mussolini, who had founded *Il Popolo d'Italia* as an interventionist newspaper in 1914. His anonymity gave him license to quote those passages of praise that the German revolutionary-conservative thinker lavished on his own leadership, emblematic of that 'Caesarism' that Spengler had announced, as far back as *Decline*, as the only political form capable of giving shape to the formless, declining world of a late 'civilisation' (as opposed to 'culture', in that key dyad for revolutionary-conservative thought). Perhaps more noteworthy, in terms of ideological divergences within the right, was Mussolini's underscoring of the incompatibility between the Spenglerian notion of race and that 'vulgar, Darwinist or materialistic spirit that is today the fashion among anti-Semites in Europe and America' – a patent dig at the new German regime whose genocidal policies he would fall in line with five years later with the promulgation of the Racial Laws, finding a common programme for the worldwide white counter-revolution.

This was not the first notable point of contact between Spengler and Mussolini. In 1928, both had written prefaces to the Italian translation of a volume by a young demographer and disciple of Spengler, Richard Korherr: *Regression of Births – Death of Peoples*.[37] Mussolini had approached Korherr via the Italian consulate after reading his work in German. Mussolini's preface, while rapping Korherr on the knuckles for imprecisions about Italian demography and echoing Spengler's glum prophecies about the effects of intellectualised megalopolitan living on the biopolitical health of nations, is notable for the centrality it accords to the looming menace posed by the 'darker nations'.[38] Foreshadowing contemporary discourse about the 'Great Replacement' and 'white genocide' – with all the brutal and useless tasks they inspire – Mussolini improbably places at the centre of his warnings about white European demographic collapse, and the 'prolific races' at its door, the example of the 'ultra-fertile' African-American population of the United States.[39] He cites a riot in Harlem in July 1927, 'barely tame' after a night of violent clashes by the police, who faced off with 'compact masses of Blacks'.[40]

Korherr's 1935 book *Denatalism: A Warning to the German People*, forecasting white decline by inference from the statistical record of ancient Rome and Greece, was prefaced by Heinrich Himmler.[41] In 1943, as the chief inspector of the statistical bureau of the SS, he delivered to Himmler a report entitled *The Final Solution to the Jewish Question*, calculating for his boss the decrease in the Jewish population in Nazi-controlled territories to date.

As *Hour of Decision* makes patent, the wordless ideas that find their non-rational reason in Spengler's nostalgic-aristocratic conception of race (as stock, breeding, superiority), are inseparable from the all-consuming, if not always nameless, fear of what white-supremacist ideologue Lothrop Stoddard – an important reference in Spengler's book – named *The Rising Tide of Color*, in explicit reaction to Du Bois's forecasts, in 'The African Roots of War', about the 'War of the Color Line'. As Spengler's 1933 text suggests, race, and especially the nebulous and all-possessing idea of whiteness, is the quintessential 'idea without words', the pulsing void at the heart of the mythological machine of the right.

7

Cathedrals of Erotic Misery[1]

Some people say to us, what I do is no one's business, it is my affair, my private life. No: anything relating to sexuality is not a private matter, but signifies the life or death of a people; world power or insignificance.

> — Heinrich Himmler, wedding speech[2]

The most urgent task of the man of steel is to pursue, to dam in and to subdue any force that threatens to transform him back into the horribly disorganized jumble of flesh, hair, skin, bones, intestines, and feelings that calls itself human.

> — Klaus Theweleit, *Male Fantasies, vol. 2 —*
> *Male Bodies: Psychoanalyzing the White Terror*

The erotics of power

At different junctures in this book, I have made a plea for turning to the 'new fascism' debates of the late 1960s and 1970s to illuminate our own political and theoretical predicament. This is perhaps even more vital in considering fascism's sexual (after)lives, since the cultural revolutions and liberationist drives of the 1960s were not only negatively constitutive of the new fascisms and anti-fascisms of their time, but they remain a crucial component in the far right's own master narratives – where 'gender ideology' is to the Stonewall Riots what 'critical race theory' is to Black Power, namely a mainstreamed, elite-supported global strategy to abolish the family, tradition and the (white) West. A planetary moral panic around transness has joined racist narratives of migration as ethnic substitution in a wellspring of fascistic energies.[3] As I argue in this chapter, theorising the vexed entanglements of fascism and eros is important as such, but it is especially urgent today, when international networks of reaction cohere around the menace posed by gender-nonconformity, and when the counterfeiting of sex and gender crises allows the geopolitical and civilisational to be mapped onto the body at its most material but also its most symbolic.

Speaking at the Schizo-Culture conference held in New York City in 1975, Michel Foucault articulated the task of thinking fascism after the 1960s in the following terms:

> I think that what has happened since 1960 is characterized by the appearance of new forms of fascism, new forms of fascist consciousness, new forms of description of fascism, and new forms of the fight against fascism. And the role of the intellectual, since the sixties, has been precisely to situate, in terms of his or her own experiences, competence, personal choices, desire – situate him or herself in such a way as to both make apparent forms of fascism which are unfortunately not recognized, or too easily tolerated, to describe them, to try to render them intolerable, and to define the specific form of struggle that can be undertaken against fascism.[4]

Like George Jackson, whose assassination had earlier been the focus of a pamphlet by the Group for Information on Prisons animated by Foucault, at the Schizo-Culture conference the French philosopher centred carceral and punitive society in his inquiries into the new forms of fascism.[5] On the same panel, R. D. Laing spoke of the political use of tranquillisers as 'drugs of conditionability', while Weather Underground prison activist Judy Clark presented a detailed account of so-called 'behaviour modification', namely the 'physical and psychological terror against people who are organizing inside [prisons] and rebelling against the conditions inside'.[6] Foucault himself elaborated upon the role of doctors in overseeing torture under the military dictatorship in Brazil.

But developing the organs to discern the unrecognised and tolerated variants of fascism, to make them both perceptible and intolerable, also meant contending with the spectacular and sexualised visibility of a certain fascism in '70s culture. Cinema in particular had become the terrain for a phantasmatic return of fascism as a sexual phenomenon in much-discussed works, from Liliana Cavani's *The Night Porter* to Pier Paolo Pasolini's *Salò*, and from Tinto Brass's *Salon Kitty* to the plethora of Nazisploitation films. It was in two interviews with French film journals in the mid-1970s that Foucault made some of his most suggestive and incisive comments on Nazism and fascism. His remarks open lines of inquiry that in many ways exceed the 'biopolitical' frame that led him, in the first volume of the *History of Sexuality*, to trace the continuities between welfare and genocide as interlinked poles of a politics of populations – in terms that remain deeply influential on current theoretical debates.

Confronted with the phantasmagorical merger in popular culture of excessive sexuality and Nazism, Foucault's first inclination is provocatively to de-eroticise fascism. As he tells his interviewer:

> Nazism was not invented by the great erotic madmen of the twentieth century but by the most sinister, boring and disgusting petit-bourgeois imaginable. Himmler was a vaguely agricultural type, and married a nurse. We must understand that the concentration camps were born from the conjoined imagination of a hospital nurse and a chicken farmer. A hospital plus a chicken coop: that's the phantasm behind the concentration camps. Millions of people were murdered there, so I don't say it to diminish the blame of those responsible for it, but precisely to disabuse those who want to

superimpose erotic values upon it. The Nazis were charwomen in the bad sense of the term. They worked with brooms and dusters, wanting to purge society of everything they considered unsanitary, dusty, filthy: syphilitics, homosexuals, Jews, those of impure blood, Blacks, the insane. It's the foul petit-bourgeois dream of racial hygiene that underlies the Nazi dream. Eros is absent.[7]

The libidinal aestheticisation of Nazism coursing through 1970s cinema and popular culture (recall David Bowie's infamous 1976 *Playboy* interview with its comments on Hitler as a rock star 'quite as good as Jagger', or the swastikas flaunted by Siouxsie Sioux and Sid Vicious) is symptomatic for Foucault of an abiding if anachronistic attraction for an eroticism proper to the disciplinary society – 'a regulated, anatomical, hierarchical society whose time is carefully distributed, its spaces partitioned, characterised by obedience and surveillance'. The name for that disciplinary eros is Sade – but, Foucault retorts: 'He bores us. He's a disciplinarian, a sergeant of sex, an accountant of the ass and its equivalents.'[8]

If, in the aftermath of 1968, the problem, as Foucault intimated in his preface to the English-language translation of *Anti-Oedipus*, was to outline the ethical protocols for a 'non-fascist life', then this also required forgetting Sade and the sordid fantasies of control his name had come to sanction. As Foucault enjoins: 'We must invent with the body, with its elements, surfaces, volumes, and thicknesses, a non-disciplinary eroticism: that of a body in a volatile and diffused state, with its chance encounters and unplanned pleasures.'[9] Or, to quote Jordy Rosenberg's recent invitation: 'If the Nazi dances all night, then our resistance requires something other than logic; something other, too, than cultured tsking or frantic bursts of wheel-spinning panic. We need desire – that messy, sometimes un-gentle, self-shattering descent into the underside of reason.'[10] The experimental invention of other, undisciplined pleasures is the obverse of the diagnosis of new, inapparent forms of fascism that eschew explicitly political or historically recognisable guises. Though ultimately preferring the register of an ethics of pleasures to that of a schizoanalysis of desires, Foucault was also preoccupied, as were Deleuze and Guattari, with what he termed 'the fascism in us all, in our heads and everyday behavior, the fascism that causes us to love power, to desire the very thing that dominates and exploits'.[11] In the 'new fascism' debates of the 1960s and 1970s, this everyday, unconscious, intimate fascism gained considerable prominence, not least, as Foucault's preface and Deleuze and Guattari's critique of left groupuscules suggest, as a (self-)critique of authoritarian relations within supposedly revolutionary collectives.[12] That is how we also find it among Black feminists in the United States. Robin Kelley cites the following passage from a section on 'The Revolt of Black Women' in the collectively authored 1973 book *Lessons from the Damned*: 'Inside families and inside us we have found the seeds of fascism that the traditional left does not want to see. Fascism was no big, frightening issue for us. It was our daily life.'[13]

The new forms of fascism of which Foucault spoke, irreducible to the repetition of organisational models and symbols from the interwar period, required a microphysics of power. By contrast with the massiveness of their 'totalitarian' forebears, these new strains of the Nazi 'brown plague' were 'microfascisms' which, in order to be properly diagnosed and disactivated, demanded an analysis of the new forms of capitalist accumulation and subjectivation. As Félix Guattari remarked:

Capitalism mobilizes everything to halt the proliferation and the actualization of unconscious potentialities. In other words, the antagonisms that Freud points out, between desire investments and superego investments, have nothing to do with a topic, nor a dynamic, but with politics and micropolitics. This is where the molecular revolution begins: you are a fascist or a revolutionary with yourself first, on the level of your superego, in relation to your body, your emotions, your husband, your wife, your children, your colleagues, in your relation to justice and the State. There is a

continuum between these 'prepersonal' domains and the infrastructures and strata that 'exceed' the individual.[14]

Guattari's formula resonates with Foucault's entreaty, quoted
above, to make detectable and intolerable those latent and tolerated
forms of fascism that lurk beneath the social threshold of recognition. It also speaks to the objective of so many post-war inquiries
into the psychic life of power under capitalism, from *The Authoritarian Personality* onward, namely to fashion a political prophylaxis
that would pre-empt the crystallisation of novel macro forms of
fascism from their largely undetected existence in the social body.
As Guattari declares: 'The microfascist elements in all our relations
with others must be found, because when we fight on the molecular
level, we'll have a much better chance of preventing a truly fascist,
a macrofascist formation on the molar level.'[15] Whence the proposal
that the organised military and party-political forms of classical
antifascism must be relayed by a 'micropolitical antifascist struggle',
which requires new clinical and critical modalities of vigilance that
move beyond only recognising fascism when it parades about in its
morbid regalia.[16] As Guattari warns:

> We must abandon, once and for all, the quick and easy formula:
> 'Fascism will not make it again.' Fascism has already 'made it', and
> it continues to 'make it'. It passes through the tightest mesh; it is in
> constant evolution, to the extent that it shares in a micropolitical
> economy of desire itself inseparable from the evolution of the pro-
> ductive forces. Fascism seems to come from the outside, but it finds
> its energy right at the heart of everyone's desire.[17]

In the context of his influential dialogue with Foucault on
'Intellectuals and Power', Deleuze had forcefully reiterated the
methodological principle that a materialist study of power, and
particularly of its fascist assemblages, cannot remain confined to
the dimension of interests – into which it is corralled by everyone

from rational-choice theorists to traditional Marxists – but must attend to 'investments of desire that function in a more profound and diffuse manner than our interests dictate'. A libidinal political materialism has to target the articulation of desires and interests, since, as Deleuze observes:

> We never desire against our interests, because interest always follows and finds itself where desire has placed it. We cannot shut out the scream of Wilhelm Reich: the masses were not deceived; at a particular time, they actually wanted a fascist regime! There are investments of desire that mold and distribute power, that make it the property of the policeman as much as of the prime minister; in this context, there is no qualitative difference between the power wielded by the policeman and the prime minister. The nature of these investments of desire in a social group explains why political parties or unions, which might have or should have revolutionary investments in the name of class interests, are so often reform oriented or absolutely reactionary on the level of desire.[18]

Deleuze's remarks about the libidinal investments that underlie police and political power are worth keeping in mind in thinking through how Foucault approached the link between power and Eros in his observations on sex and Nazism on screen.

If Foucault's first move is to deflate the prurient conceit of a sexually transgressive, Sadean fascism, he also takes these sexualised forgeries of memory and meaning as the occasion to sketch out an account of power's 'erotic charge'. The sheer unlikelihood of a Nazi eroticism is a historical and political quandary that demands our attention:

> How is it that Nazism – which was represented by shabby, pathetic puritanical characters, laughably Victorian old maids, or at best, smutty individuals – how has it now managed to become, in France, in Germany, in the United States, in all pornographic literature

throughout the world, the ultimate symbol of eroticism? Every shoddy erotic fantasy is now attributed to Nazism. Which raises a fundamentally serious problem: how do you love power? ... What leads to power being desirable, and to actually being desired? It's easy to see the process by which this eroticising is transmitted, reinforced, etc. But for the eroticising to work, it's necessary that the attachment to power, the acceptance of power by those over whom it is exerted, is already erotic.[19]

The Nazi sexploitation film appears then as a symptom of a contemporaneous collapse in the erotic attachment to power ('Nobody loves power any more ... obviously you can't be in love with Brezhnev, Pompidou or Nixon') and of fledgling efforts to re-eroticise power, ranging from 'porn-shops with Nazi insignia' to then French President Valery Giscard d'Estaing's penchant for stylish lounge suits.

But Foucault also excavates the sources of power's erotic charge in the political organisation of fascist violence, in a manner that arguably moves beyond the dialectic of desire and interest and sheds light on what we discussed in an earlier chapter in the guise of 'fascist freedom'. Here, the polemic against Marxists' treatment of fascism pivots on the claim (true of Georgi Dimitrov and his epigones, not so of Guérin or Bloch) that their figuration of fascist rule as the exacerbation of bourgeois dictatorship neglects crucial elements of its composition and functioning. In particular, Foucault contends:

It leaves out the fact that Nazism and fascism were only possible insofar as there could exist within the masses a relatively large section which took on the responsibility for a number of state functions of repression, control, policing, etc. This, I believe, is a crucial characteristic of Nazism; that is, its deep penetration inside the masses and the fact that a part of the power was actually delegated to a specific fringe of the masses. This is where the word 'dictatorship' becomes true in general, and relatively false. When you think of the power an individual could possess under a Nazi regime as soon as he was simply S.S. or signed up in the Party! You could actually kill your neighbor, steal his wife, his house![20]

As in Johann Chapoutot's account of Nazi management theories as paeans to the autonomy of performance and initiative, what we encounter in Foucault's observations is a powerful challenge to the commonplace that fascism is fundamentally defined by a centralisation and concentration of power. For Foucault, to the extent that there is an eroticisation of power under Nazism, it is conditioned by a logic of delegation, deputising and decentralisation of what remains in form and content a vertical, exclusionary and murderous kind of power. Fascism is not just the apotheosis of the leader above the sheeplike masses of his followers; it is also, in a less spectacular but perhaps more consequential manner, the reinvention of the settler logic of petty sovereignty, a highly conditional but very real 'liberalising' and 'privatising' of the monopoly of violence. As Foucault tells his interviewer:

> You have to bear in mind the way power was delegated, distributed within the very heart of the population; you have to bear in mind this vast transfer of power that Nazism carried out in a society like Germany. It's wrong to say that Nazism was the power of the great industrialists carried on under a different form. It wasn't simply the intensified central power of the military – it was that, but only on one particular level ... Nazism never gave people any material advantages, it never handed out any thing but power ... The fact is that contrary to what is usually understood by dictatorship – the power of a single person – you could say that in this kind of regime the most repulsive (but in a sense the most intoxicating) part of power was given to a considerable number of people. The SS was that which was given the power to kill, to rape.[21]

Foucault's insight into the 'erotics' of a power based on the deputising of violence is a more fecund frame, I would argue, for the analysis of both classical and late fascisms than Guattari's hyperbolic claim that 'the masses invested a fantastic collective death instinct in ... the fascist machine' – which misses out on the materiality of that 'transfer of power' to a '*specific* fringe of the masses' that Foucault diagnosed as critical to fascism's desirability.[22]

The gendering of the fascist libido is largely neglected or implicitly presupposed in the arguments by Foucault, Deleuze and Guattari we've just considered. Answering their theoretical challenge while largely jettisoning their attention to the political economy and power structures of fascism, in his *Male Fantasies* Klaus Theweleit centres the palingenetic misogyny and paranoid body politics of fascism – the 'Red Woman' as a psychosomatic menace of dissolution warranting murderous rage, a damming of the flood – to grasp how desiring production could morph into death production.[23] In the context of today's noxious commingling of fascisation with new bands of brothers (*Männerbunde*), physical or virtual, Theweleit has inspired the exploration of contemporary microfascism as a 'war of restoration' that seeks to revive an archaic fantasy of patriarchal power by enacting violent practices of 'autogenetic sovereignty' – the reproduction of male power without and against women.[24] As Jack Z. Bratich argues: 'The palingenetic project of masculine rebirth seeks a future without bio-reproduction. It populates the world with martyrs and myths, the ghostly squads of past and future. It is a replication without reproduction.'[25] And yet, because

> the autogenetic sovereign is always an impossible project, it needs continuous renewal, and it recommences world-making via policing, punishment, and control ... we are faced with a double move by the autogenetic sovereign: a flight from dependence while returning to depend on women.[26]

This impossibility could also be approached in terms of the *discontinuity* between the sources of fascism in male groups bonded by practices and/or fantasies of violence, on the one hand, and on the other, fascism as a project for reconfiguring state and society, which must perforce incorporate and interpellate women after its own fashion.

Emancipation from emancipation: women and fascism

The Parisian theoretical debate of the 1970s on the new forms of fascism did not simply bypass the question of women, fascism and desire. The Italian journalist, academic and Communist parliamentarian Maria Antonietta Macciocchi organised a seminar at Paris VIII University in Vincennes with an impressive range of speakers who brought post-'68 politics and high theory to bear on the history and future of fascism (among them Nicos Poulantzas on the popular impact of fascism, Jean Toussaint Desanti on Giovanni Gentile and fascism's philosophical origins and Jean-Pierre Faye on fascism and language).[27] The seminar also featured screenings of fascist and anti-fascist films, from Veit Harlan's anti-Semitic production *Jud Süss* to Luchino Visconti's *Ossessione*, from Nico Naldini's *Fascista* to Roberto Rossellini's *La Nave Bianca*. It was also the occasion for ideological clashes with and physical disruptions by Maoist activists from the Groupe Foudre, led by Natacha Michel, who saw Macciocchi as the purveyor of a reactionary theory of sexo-fascism, which obscured class and capital for the sake of an anti-Marxist libidinal framework.[28] Macciocchi made a number of contributions to the seminar, most significant of which was a long essay on women and fascism, which would later be published in Italian and part of which appeared in English translation as 'Female Sexuality in Fascist Ideology'.[29]

For Macciocchi, the nexus of women and fascism — women's interpellation by, participation in and even desire for fascism — had become a kind feminist taboo, the blind spot of a feminist movement that tended to treat women just like a *gauchiste* ultra-left treated the proletariat: hagiographically, as a kind of fetish beyond reproach.[30] While anchoring her analysis in a plenteous archive of textual materials from the fascist *ventennio*, Macciocchi also made ample use of Wilhelm Reich's theories on the libidinal infrastructure of fascist power. Sex in general, and women's sexuality in particular, was subjected by fascism to a concerted strategy of expropriation. As Macciocchi declared: 'In fascism sexuality, like wealth, belongs to a powerful oligarchy. The masses are dispossessed of both.'[31] Fascist mass dictatorship, following Reich, was seen as grounded in 'a huge sexual repression which is tightly linked to death', while in the Italian case, building on Catholic tradition, it invented a particularly potent cocktail of reproductive normativity and what we've encountered in Furio Jesi as a *religio mortis*, a religion of death.[32] 'The characteristic of fascist and Nazi genius', writes Macciocchi, 'is their challenge to women on their own ground: they make women both the reproducers of life and the guardians of death, without the two terms being contradictory.'[33] The nationalisation of both family and sex makes possible a biopolitics of reproduction that is also a necropolitics (*Viva la muerte!*). Not just breeding sons for the front – or daughters who in turn will make more sons for future fronts – the fascist woman is also enlisted in a libidinised religion of death that glorifies the national martyr, fallen in the act of killing. Conversely, the reterritorialization of sex onto the nationalised family, both materially and symbolically, plays a crucial ideological role. As Macciocchi affirms: 'The "emotional" plague of fascism is spread through an epidemic of familialism.'[34]

In brief, 'You can't talk about fascism unless you are also prepared to discuss patriarchy.'[35] In her introduction to the publication of Macciocchi's article in the first issue of *Feminist Review*, the historian Jane Caplan helpfully summarised the theory of ideology that lay at the core of its theses:

> Fascism enlists the support of women by addressing them in an ideological-sexual language with which they are already familiar through the 'discourses' of bourgeois Christian ideology. In abstract terms, this is to say that the system of signs and unconscious

representations which constitute the 'law' of patriarchy is invoked
in fascist ideology in such a way that women are drawn into a particular supportive relation with fascist regimes: indeed, Macciocchi
even seems to suggest that this 'availability' of women is also constitutive of fascism, and is not just a passive reservoir ... so long as
women continue to allow themselves to be addressed in the patriarchal language of sexual alienation, they will remain a potential
audience for the persuasions of fascism.[36]

But Caplan also voiced some astute criticisms about this framing of
the problem of women under fascism. Macciocchi sometimes fell
prey to the eclectic fallacy: because fascism is a scavenger ideology
cobbling together available ideological elements, there is a temptation to treat each of those elements (rather than the specificity of each
element's incorporation and articulation into a broader ensemble)
as itself fascist or proto-fascist. Caplan also queried the opposition,
which this book has already touched upon, of (irrational) desires
and (rational) interests, while casting doubt on suggestions that
there existed a *sui generis* feminine enthusiasm for fascism. Hers is
also a plea for a materialist and historical analysis by contrast with
an unchecked use of psychoanalytic categories:

> The sphere of ideology/the unconscious risks becoming a country
> in which *everything* is said to be possible, a kind of comprehensive
> and privileged residual category with boundaries that fade into
> indistinct horizons. This seems to court the danger of ascribing to
> fascism an ultimate and exclusive capacity to dominate an other-
> wise impregnable terrain; of proposing the unconscious as the
> proper and peculiar domain of fascism, without suggesting, beyond
> a handful of arcane allusions, how this is to be recaptured.[37]

To Caplan's caveats we could add that viewing fascism through the
prism of the sexually repressive family can have distorting effects.
While avoiding the prurient image of fascism as sexual perversion,

the diametrically opposed notion that 'the body of fascist discourse is rigorously chaste, pure, virginal' and that its 'central aim is the death of sexuality' is contradicted by the historical record of fascist sex policies.[38]

As the historian Dagmar Herzog demonstrated in her brilliant study *Sex After Fascism*, the identification of fascism with sexual repression was in part a by-product of a sixties reaction against a complicit post-war establishment (the parents' generation), which had itself imposed sexual and moral conservatism as a bulwark against fascism's subversions of the traditional family (and to disavow its own earlier participation in the regime). Sexualised interpretations of Nazism had their own history and periodisation, conditioned by the moral and political conflicts in their own moment. As Herzog notes, in early 1950s Germany

> commentators still emphasised Nazism's anti-bourgeois component and explicitly linked Nazi encouragements to nonmarital sexuality with Nazism's crimes [while] the Auschwitz trial of 1963-5 in Frankfurt am Main marked the emergence of the theory of the petty bourgeois and sexually repressed Holocaust perpetrator that was to become so important to the new Left movement.[39]

Neither great erotic madmen nor petty bourgeois charwomen, the Nazis advanced a politics of sex that cannot be reduced to prior models of sexual regulation (bourgeois or petty bourgeois, liberal or conservative), or to a generic patriarchy; following Herzog, we can see it as a mobile synthesis between, on the one hand, a pragmatic moral conservatism and, on the other, the acceleration of modernising sexual trends in a racist and nationalist guise. *Pace* Theweleit, 'the core of all fascist propaganda' is *not* 'a battle against everything that constitutes enjoyment and pleasure'.[40] As Herzog argues:

> When the Nazis came to power in 1933, they frequently presented themselves to the public as restorers of traditional sexual morality

(although this stance was also contested within the party leadership quite early on). And yet, as the Third Reich unfolded, a wholly new and highly racialised sexual politics emerged. While sexually conservative appeals continued to be promoted to the very end, it became clear that under Nazism many (though certainly not all) preexisting liberalizing trends would be deliberately intensi-fied, even as, simultaneously, sexual freedom and happiness were redefined as solely the prerogatives of 'healthy' 'Aryan' hetero-sexuals.[41]

With its grounding in a sub-Nietzschean critique of the Christian repression of the body, its sources in the myriad naturisms, nudisms and body cults that traversed early twentieth-century Germany, and its obsession with the martial aestheticisation of the body in ancient Greece and Rome (reinterpreted as Mediterranean outposts of the Nordic race), Nazism cannot therefore be reduced to petty bourgeois repression.[42] Its 'familialism' should also not be merely chalked up to the hunger for young cannon-fodder or white-supremacist phantasmagorias; it was also, as the historian Tim Mason detailed in a bravura essay on women under National Socialism, a function of German fascism's encounter with the cultural and material con-tradictions of capitalism. The family could appear as a kind of *fix*, but also as a site of psychological and material compromise between an anxious population and a regime devoid of any 'middle ground between dramatic and brutal improvisation on the one hand and the pursuit of visionary final goals on the other'.[43] As Mason concluded, the Nazis'

propaganda and their policies magnified the much more fundamen-tal *reconciliatory function* of family life, and people were responsive to this because [it] spoke to long-established and almost universal mechanisms of self-protection against the alienated rigours of life outside the home ... The nightmare world of dictatorial govern-ment, huge industrial combines, all-encompassing administration

and organized inhumanity was parasitic upon its ideological antithesis, the minute community of parents and children.[44]

Yet in spite of its tendentious and eclectic overemphasis on certain
dimension of the sexual life of fascism, Macciocchi's work remains
important for its contention that the problem of fascism and women
(and fascism and gender more broadly) cannot be evaded. As she
admonishes:

> If the past (and present?) relationship between women and fascist
> ideology is not analysed, if we do not analyse how and why fascism
> has fooled women, then feminism itself (and likewise the entire
> political vanguard) will remain deprived of an understanding of
> its historical context. Without this dialectical analysis feminism
> is mutilated; it is suspended without a past, like a timeless hot-air
> balloon, and can understand neither what is at stake today nor the
> direction of any future alliance between feminist and revolutionary
> struggle.[45]

Among the dialectical objects of such an analysis is the consolidation under fascism of a 'female antifeminism', the product of what
Macciocchi perceptively terms the '*antipolitical politicisation*' of
women by fascist and Nazi regimes.[46] As Robyn Marasco has argued,
in an insightful critical recovery of Macciocchi's work alongside
Andrea Dworkin's writings on ultra-right women activists in the
United States, notwithstanding its limitations, this work can trouble
aseptic, disembodied analyses of fascism as a 'purely' political phenomenon and attune us to the role of gender, sexuality and sex in
contemporary processes of fascisation. As Marasco, rhetorically, asks:

> On an even more basic level, can we speak of the fascisation
> without speaking of sex? Will we be in any position to understand
> the fascism of our present and how it relates to fascisms past? Will
> we understand how online misogyny becomes [a] gateway drug to

[the] Far Right, how the world of men's rights activists, pick-up artists, MGTOW trolls, and 'involuntary celibates' overlaps with that of white supremacists, militia men, and proud boys, or even how a relatively minor episode like #gamergate could be plausibly described one of the inaugural events of the Trump era? Will we recognise in the 'Great Replacement' myth a bid for control of women's sexuality, as well as racist and culturalist panic? Even more to my point here, without seeing sex as an instrument of fascisation, can we make sense of the anti-vaxxers, yoga moms, and wellness gurus who are part of the new Right resurgence, how the Q-anon conspiracy mobilises women's fears for their children?[47]

But while the response may be an emphatic yes, this does not mean that the sexed and gendered patterns of fascisation will take familiar forms. Indeed, anchoring her reflections in the case of Ashli Babbitt, 'martyr' of the January 6 'insurrection', Marasco enjoins us to think to the regressive forms of empowerment and the transgressive pleasures that may be afforded certain women in contemporary far-right movements. What fascistic right-wing scenes offer may not primarily be patriarchal security (though its pastiche is on offer for 'tradwives' and their kind). Rather, it may be

something more immediately transgressive, more responsive to destructive impulses and antisocial forces, and more proximate to the equality that it rejects and the freedom it renounces. It offers white women an account of their unhappiness and an affective arena to express their rage ... It is not simply a question of protecting one's interests (as white women, petit-bourgeois women, women with American citizenship), or even desiring one's own domination, but of gaining access to the pleasures of 'masculine' affect and agency. It is a privilege reserved only for some women, which is part of the point. And it is a form of 'female antifeminism' that mirrors the neoliberal feminism it opposes, another degraded version of *having it all*, where instead of the corporate career and the heterosexual reproductive family, women can have combat training, AR 15s, polyamorous sexuality, conspiracism, and, above all, a semblance of power that substitutes for the real thing.[48]

This recomposition of female antifeminism can also shade into a 'fascist feminism', which seeks to violently secure and affirm a normative, if not necessarily heteropatriarchal, figure of woman, and which invests desire and libido in its narratives about the imminent threat of the erasure of women and even feminism by 'gender ideology' and transness.[49]

Sex in crisis

Fascism advertises itself as the solution, the fix, to a comprehensive crisis of order. Not just social order, but order across all its semantic and material registers: economic, geopolitical, spiritual, aesthetic, corporeal, racial. And sexual. From the fascist vantage, organic crisis is always a crisis of the organic, a deregulation of the senses, a disorder in our organs. But unlike reactionary conservatisms, which it ably manipulates, fascism is never merely reducible to a desire for restoration, putting bodies back in their proper place.[50] Aware, if not always avowing, that the path to a lost harmony is irreparably blocked, fascism's forward-flight into the past is inevitably accompanied by all kinds of recombinant inventions, conservative revolutions that affect reproduction and sexuality, desire and pleasure, the intimate and the collective. In this domain too, if fascism repeats, it does so with a difference. We are not done with the politically engineered panics around (Jewish) racial defilement, the 'crisis-woman' and homosexuality that shaped interwar European fascisms, or the gendering of racial fascism's terror-laden regulation of Blackness and colonial subalternity which both preceded and outlived the Rome-Berlin Axis.[51] But we also have to contend with new forms of fascism (including everyday fascisms and microfascisms) emerging from the transformations in the realms of sex, gender and sexuality, and from the mutable articulations between the libidinal, the economic and the natural.

As scholars of the far right's recompositions in the context of climate emergency have observed, reactionary sexual and gender norms don't just map onto a domestic or intimate sphere but are also antagonistic mediations of the social totality, responsive to imaginaries of the social (and natural) whole. As Cara Daggett suggests, the aggressive nostalgia for an obsolescent assemblage of maleness, motoring and manufacture – which transcends the historical heartlands of Fordism – can be grasped as the consolidation of a *petro-masculinity*, alerting us

> to the possibility that climate change can catalyse fascist desires to secure a *lebensraum*, a living space, a household that is barricaded from the spectre of threatening others, whether pollutants or immigrants or gender deviants. Taking petro-masculinity seriously means paying attention to the thwarted desires of privileged patriarchies as they lose their fossil fantasies.[52]

This embattled loss of fantasy (and fantasy of loss) by 'an increasingly fragile Western hypermasculinity' can also be figured as a theft of enjoyment – which, if we keep in mind the exploitative and extractive history of those colonial, racial and patriarchal histories, is perhaps more accurately described as the *theft of the enjoyment of theft* (and of the order emerging from and reproduced by plunder). The thieves of enjoyment may take multiple, varying, incoherent forms (predatory Jewish plutocrats, Prius-driving metropolitan liberal elites, Black welfare mothers, trans women), but for the fascist imaginary, without their removal or repression, no 'institutionalised rebirth', no restorative revolution, is possible.[53]

As feminist and queer anti-fascists have long argued, fascisms are not just racial regimes but also sexual and gender regimes.[54] The antipolitical politicisation of sex and gender plays a critical role in the formation and circulation of fascism. It invests the experience of crisis at its most intimate and visceral, where social and economic disorders seemingly too abstract to be mapped make themselves felt in domestic, libidinal and bodily registers. Late fascism is both a libidinal proposition – a claim staked on collective desires – and a sex panic, or better, a gender panic. Right-wing culture today is the culture of uncivil wars that frontstage the regulation, targeting and stigmatisation of sexed and sexual bodies. It is also a disturbingly transnational, 'viral' culture, in which the repair and reinvention of a martial masculinity and the anxious nostalgia for the heteronormative family as the cell-form of the *demos* and *ethnos* are the foci around which an entire institutional and ideological infrastructure is cohering, with 'gender ideology' and transness as nemeses. If 'gender-critical activism functions … as a large-scale translation process through which particular counter-theories and concepts are formulated and released into [global] circulation', it is not only because of its capacity to create novel articulations between conservative and feminist formations, but because it presents gender trouble as global crisis, both spawn and vector of a bad, globalist capitalism, directed by deracinated elites colluding with deviant and subaltern subjects to further dispossess already precarious 'ordinary citizens' – creating what Serena Bassi and Greta LaFleur have provocatively dubbed 'a postfascist feminism of the 99 percent'.[55]

Fascism's antipolitics of sex is a strategy, as Himmler's wedding speech grimly reminds us, for tying the geopolitical to the genital (as well as the genomic or the hormonal). It is, in a sense, not surprising, though no less grotesque, that late fascism frequently coheres and circulates around the moral panic about transness and 'gender ideology'. There is a kind of sexual and gender 'scalarity' at work here: not only does the thematising of sex-gender disorder allow a projection of 'macro' troubles to 'micro' scales – the imminent end of Western civilisation is inscribed on unruly bodies – but the consolidation of a new 'Fascist international', and its capacity to capture and hegemonise older conservatisms, takes place largely through the lens of a planetary crisis in gender and sex norms.[56]

This has served to cement political infrastructures and solidarities among disparate political subjects, all committed to the idea that we are in the midst of a cultural world war in which queerness and transness are the harbingers of a civilisational collapse that must be thwarted at all costs.[57] Where the migrant of colour is the avatar of the Great Replacement, the eventual extinction of whiteness and its component nations, transness is the emblem and emissary of a Great Disorder, the scrambling of sexual difference and the destruction of the family. If the fascisms born out of the killing fields of the First World War tried to project the logic of the front onto social and sexual crises — fighting Red, female and Jewish masses as vectors of dissolution of the body's very boundaries — today's late fascisms, largely unmoored from 'war as inner experience' but ardently nostalgic for martial masculinities, fixate on gender nonconformity as both metaphor and metonymy, cause and symptom of a disorder at scales both personal and planetary.[58] For them, the decline of the West *is* gender trouble, and the contagious desire for a better life beyond hierarchies of racial identity and sexual normality is an illness, a social pathology, the deviant dystopia against which to erect the regressive image of a life of incessant struggle and the desperate desire for a tradition to come.[59]

Conclusion

This book is the product of an effort to think fascism as a process and potential haunting a world riven and unsettled by multiple overlapping crises. Drawing on the rich archives of anti-fascist thought, I have sought to theorise fascism's social and ideological dynamics, its cultures and temporalities, rather than naming or classifying movements, regimes or individuals. I have tried to approach the relationship between historical fascism and contemporary signs of fascisation, not analogically by comparing epigones to an exemplar, but contrapuntally, allowing history and the present to illuminate, but also unsettle, one another. This has also meant foregrounding those features of interwar European fascism that exceed the frames of canonical interpretations to resonate with our own historical moment – for instance, by reflecting on fascism's deviations from our common sense about a total state based on snuffing out all liberty and autonomy.

Fiercely, viciously identitarian, fascism also evades exhaustive identification. It repeats, but with differences, scavenging the ideological terrain for usable materials – not uncommonly from its antagonists on the left. It can flaunt its relativism while trading in absolutes. And for all its Cold War association with the hyper-statist logic of totalitarianism, it breeds its own forms of pluralism and its own visions of freedom. My wager has been that it is possible to think cogently about the elements of fascism as an anti-emancipatory politics of crisis without equating theory and definition, avoiding the checklist of tell-tale features or the streamlined schedule of the steps to fascist victory. A critical theory of fascism need not take the form of a diagnostic and statistical manual of political disorders.

The radical theorists of racial and colonial fascism that have anchored my own reflections in these pages, as well as my criticisms of historical analogy, can attune us to four interlocking dimensions of the history and experience of fascism.

The first is that the practices and ideologies that crystallised, more or less laboriously, into Italian fascism, German Nazism and their European kin were presaged and prepared by the dispossession and exploitation of 'lesser breeds without the Law' wrought by settler-colonialism, chattel slavery and intra-European racial capitalism (or internal colonialism). It is one of this book's wagers that our 'late' fascism cannot be understood without the 'fascisms before fascism' that accompanied the imperialist consolidation of a capitalist world-system.

Second, fascism has been differentially applied, experienced and named across axes of race, gender and sexuality. As we learn from the writings of incarcerated revolutionaries of colour in the United States, political orders widely deemed liberal-democratic can harbour institutions that operate as regimes of domination and terror for ample sectors of their population, in something like a racial dual state.[1] This means that both in their political origins and their strategic imperatives, abolitionism and contemporary anti-fascism cannot be disjoined.

Third, fascism is grounded in a modality of preventive counter-violence, its desire for ethnonational rebirth or revanche stoked by the imminence of a threat projected as civilisational, demographic and existential. The epochal panic about the 'rising tide of colour' and the 'coloured world revolution' that seeded the rise of fascism after the First World War has morphed (barely) into narratives of replacement, substitution or cultural suicide shared by mass shooters and European prime ministers alike.

Fourth, fascism required the production of identifications and subjectivities, desires and forms of life, which do not simply demand obedience to despotic state power but draw on a *sui generis* idea of freedom. Whether in the guise of decentralised and deputised power or psychological wages, the fascist – as the phantasmatic synthesis of the settler and the soldier (or the cop) – needs to imagine him or herself as an active shareholder in the monopoly of violence as well as an enterprising petty sovereign, with race and nation serving as the affective and ideological vectors of identification with power.

If we keep these dimensions in mind – the longue durée of colonial racial capitalism, the differential experience of domination, political violence pre-empting an imagined existential threat, the subject as deputy of sovereign violence – we can begin to comprehend how contemporary fascist potentials converge and crystallise into forms of 'border fascism'. Whether that border be a physical demarcation to be walled and patrolled, or a set of fractal fault lines running through the body politic and multiply marked and policed, there is no circumventing the fact that, as 'the cycles of capitalism driving both mass migration and repression converge with the climate crisis' and a racial-civilisational crisis is spliced with scenarios of scarcity and collapse, the extreme and authoritarian right will map its politics of time – and especially its obsession with epochal loss of privilege and purity – onto the space of territory.[2] It will also, like its twentieth-century forebears, seek to gain control over the borders of the body, to patrol the demarcations between genders and sexes.

Ruth Wilson Gilmore has encapsulated the idea of racial capitalism in the formula 'capitalism requires inequality and racism enshrines it'.[3] Fascism, we could add, strives violently to enshrine inequality under conditions of crisis by creating simulacra of equality for some – it is a politics and a culture of national-social entrenchment, nourished by racism, in a situation of real or anticipated social catastrophe. As a politics of crisis, it is a limit case of 'capitalism saving capitalism from capitalism' (sometimes even creating the mirage of a capitalism without capitalism).[4] Countering the fascist potentials and processes that traverse the global present therefore cannot mean subordinating the practical critique of capitalism to watered-down (un)popular fronts with liberals or conservatives. A 'progressive' neoliberalism – the one that lies in the back of most mainstream denunciations of fascism – is defined by the production and reproduction of inequalities and exclusions inconsistently accompanied by formalistic and formulaic commitments to rights, diversity and difference. Those who make common cause with it will have to do so in the awareness that they are 'manning the imperial gates', allying with the cause to ward off its effects.[5] Whoever is not willing to talk about anti-capitalism should also keep quiet about anti-fascism. The latter, capaciously understood, is not just a matter of resisting the worst, but will always be inseparable from the collective forging of ways of living that can undo the lethal romances of identity, hierarchy and domination that capitalist crisis throws up with such grim regularity.

Acknowledgments

This book draws on some previously published material: 'Notes on Late Fascism', *Historical Materialism* (website), 2 April 2017; 'The Long Shadow of Racial Fascism', *Boston Review* 28, October 2020; 'Incipient Fascism: Black Radical Perspectives', *CLCWeb: Comparative Literature and Culture* 23: 1, 2021; 'Fascists, Freedom and the Anti-State State', *Historical Materialism* 29: 4, 2021, 3–21; 'Roundtable on Class', *ARTMargins* 10: 3, 2022; 'The Returns of Racial Fascism', in *For Antifascist Futures: Against the Violence of Imperial Crisis*, ed. Alyosha Goldstein and Simón Ventura Trujillo, Oakland: Common Notions, 2022; 'The Nightwatchman's Bludgeon', *Sidecar*, 29 October 2022.

Arguments from this book were rehearsed in dialogue at Marxism in Culture, Historical Materialism annual conferences, the Pontificia Universidad Católica de Valparaíso, the Valparaíso critical theory colloquium on 'Violence, Politics, and the Event', Red May, Foreign Objekt, Maumaus, the Program in Critical Theory at UC Berkeley, the Cologne Mythological Network, KU Leuven, the Digital Democracies Institute at Simon Fraser University and the Theory in Crisis seminar at the University of London in Paris, as well as in my undergraduate and graduate teaching at Goldsmiths, University of London and Simon Fraser University. I thank all the organisers, participants, students and workers who made these (distanced or in person) meetings, lectures and discussions possible for their time, generosity, criticism and curiosity.

Many conversations and much correspondence, commissioning and comradeship, have made this book possible. My gratitude goes to Jürgen Bock, Eugene Brennan, Sebastian Budgen, Darren Byler, Clint Burnham, Michael Carr, Zoë Druick, Ricardo Espinoza Lolas, Steve Edwards, Roderick Ferguson, Craig Gilmore, Ruth Wilson Gilmore, Alyosha Goldstein, Avery F. Gordon, Am Johal, Ken Kawashima, Stathis Kouvelakis, Andreas Malm, Matteo Mandarini, Geoff Mann, James E. Martel, Svitlana Matviyenko, Adam McGee, Toni Negri, Gabriele Pedullà, Quinn Slobodian, Jason E. Smith, Michele Spanò, Mario Telò, Massimiliano Tomba, Tom Vandeputte, Gavin Walker, Jeffery R. Webber and Evan Calder Williams. For their comments and suggestions on the draft manuscript, I am particularly indebted to Michael Hardt, Harry Harootunian, Jon Goldberg-Hiller and Brenna Bhandar. Special thanks to Jordy Rosenberg, without whom the thorny question of fascist eros and gender panic would have gone largely, and culpably, unexplored. My comradely gratitude to Rosie Warren at Verso for her careful editorial work on the manuscript and her valiant efforts to restrain the convolutions of my prose. Thanks also to Bruno George for the thoughtful copy editing.

Without the love, example and support of Francesca Lancillotti and Roberto Toscano (*il mio giusto!*) none of this would have been possible. And to Esha: *Cessa il vento, calma è la bufera.*

Notes

Preface

1   Federico Finchelstein, 'Biden Called Trumpism "Semi-Fascism." The Term Makes Sense, Historically', *The Washington Post*, 1 September 2022. 'Semi-fascist' is used repeatedly to characterise the US nativist-populist far right in leading CPUSA member William Z. Foster's 'Fascist Tendencies in the United States', originally published in October 1935 in *Communist*, now in *The US Antifascism Reader*, eds Bill V. Mullen and Christopher Vials, London: Verso, 2020, 68–87.

2   Consider also journalist Yossi Klein's acerbic reflections on the Israeli governing coalition: 'Just the way we legitimized Ben Gvir, we'll legitimize fascism. We'll convert it. We'll take the far right, put a skullcap and ritual fringes on it and we'll have Zionist-religious fascism.' 'It's Official Now: Fascism Is Us', *Haaretz*, 4 November 2022. Compare the collective letter to the *New York Times*, from 2 December 1948, signed by Hannah Arendt and Albert Einstein among others, condemning Netanyahu's political forebears in Herut as the 'latest manifestation of fascism'.

3   Ranjona Bannerji, 'Modi Govt Has Unleashed the Might and Breadth of its Fascist Vision on India', *National Herald*, 20 January 2020.

4   For the most theoretically original and politically nuanced contribution to a very uneven debate, see Ilya Budraitskis, 'Putinism: A New Form of Fascism?', *Spectre*, 27 October 2022.

5   Fredric Jameson, 'Metacommentary', *PMLA* 86: 1, 1971, 10; Theodor W. Adorno, 'Anti-Semitism and Fascist Propaganda', in *The Stars Down to*

Earth: And Other Essays on the Irrational in Culture, ed. Stephen Crook, London: Routledge, 1994, 221.

6   Kojin Karatani, 'History and Repetition in Japan', in *History and Repetition*, ed. Seiji M. Lippett, New York: Columbia University Press, 2004, 34. In the chapter on racial fascism, we will see how Angela Y. Davis advanced a similar proposition. For Karatani, seeing fascism as process also pre-empts the error of supposing that fascism must have a durable and homogeneous subject.

7   I borrow the formulation from Maria Mies's *Patriarchy and Accumulation on a World Scale*. For a compelling panorama and diagnosis of the far right's response to the climate emergency, see Sam Moore and Alex Roberts, *The Rise of Ecofascism: Climate Change and the Far Right*, Cambridge: Polity, 2022.

1. Out of Time

1   Franco 'Bifo' Berardi, 'National Workerism and Racial Warfare', *DiEM 25*, 10 November 2016, diem25.org. See also Bifo's contribution in Franco 'Bifo' Berardi, Chantal Mouffe, Wilhelm Heimeyer, G. M. Tamás, *A New Fascism?*, ed. Susanne Pfeffer, London: Koenig Books, 2018.

2   For a lucid and nuanced introduction to the Western Marxist discussion, from the standpoint of the 1970s, see Anson Rabinbach, 'Toward a Marxist Theory of Fascism and National Socialism: A Report on Developments in West Germany', *New German Critique* 3, 1974, 127–53.

3   Consider the debates of the 1930s and 1940s, especially those framed by the analyses of Frankfurt School theorists like Friedrich Pollock and Franz Neumann, over the viability of state capitalism, debates that contemporary historical work, such as Adam Tooze's *The Wages of Destruction*, continue to illuminate.

4   Oliver Cromwell Cox, *Caste, Class, and Race: A Study in Social Dynamics*, New York: Monthly Review Press, 1959 [1948], 188–9.

5   Riley notes that while there are interesting parallels between the present and the interwar period in terms of the 'politicization of intra-dominant class conflicts' (between agrarian and industrial capital back then, between extractive industries and health insurance under Trump), the political dynamics emerging from these struggles among capitalists are disanalogous. Dylan Riley, 'Introduction to the Second Edition', *The Civic Foundations of Fascism in Europe*, London: Verso, 2019, xxviii.

6   'The serious objection which I have of this book (if not of its author
    as well) is that it in absolutely no way corresponds to the conditions in
    which it appears, but rather takes its place inappropriately, like a great
    lord, who arriving at the scene of an area devastated by an earthquake
    can find nothing more urgent to do than to spread out the Persian carpets
    – which by the way are already somewhat moth-eaten – and to display
    the somewhat tarnished golden and silver vessels, and the already faded
    brocade and damask garments which his servants had brought.' Walter
    Benjamin, Letter to Alfred Cohn of 6 February 1935, cited in Anson
    Rabinbach, 'Unclaimed Heritage: Ernst Bloch's *Heritage of Our Times*
    and the Theory of Fascism', *New German Critique* 11, 1977, 5.

7   As Rabinbach perceptively notes, highlighting the significance of
    Benjamin's reflections on capitalism, technology and modern specta-
    cle: 'Bloch emphasizes the continuity between fascism and the tradition
    embodied in its ideas, but he neglects those elements of discontinuity
    with the past – elements which give fascism its unique power as a form of
    social organization – so that its actual links to modern capitalism remain
    obscure.' Ibid., 14.

8   Ernst Bloch, 'Nonsynchronism and the Obligation to Its Dialectics',
    trans. M. Ritter, *New German Critique* 11, 1977, 26. This text is excerpted
    from *Heritage of Our Times*. It is fruitful to compare these observations
    with Tosaka Jun's contemporaneous (1935) reflections on Japanese
    'emperor-fascism' and its 'restorationist' agenda: Tosaka Jun, 'The Fate
    of Japanism: From Fascism to Emperorism', in *Tosaka Jun: A Critical
    Reader*, trans. John Person, eds Ken C. Kawashima, Fabian Schäfer, and
    Robert Stolz, Ithaca, NY: Cornell East Asia Series, 2013, 65, 67.

9   Bloch, *The Heritage of Our Times*, quoted in Rabinbach, 'Unclaimed
    Heritage', 13–14.

10 Rabinbach, 'Unclaimed Heritage', 7.

11 Bloch, 'Uber Ungleichzeitigkeit, Provinz und Propaganda, Ein Gesprich
    mit Rainer Traub und Harald Wieser', quoted in Rabinbach, 'Unclaimed
    Heritage', 16.

12 Pier Paolo Pasolini, 'Il vuoto di potere in Italia', *Il Corriere della Sera*, 10
    February 1975. The article would later be reprinted in *Scritti corsari*, a
    collection of Pasolini's journalistic interventions published shortly after
    his death.

13 John Brenkman, 'Introduction to Bataille', *New German Critique* 16, 1979,
    62. Brenkman also makes the affinities with Bloch explicit, while arguing

for the abiding relevance of these heterodox theorists to 1970s debates on fascism.

14   Georges Bataille, 'The Psychological Structure of Fascism', trans. Carl L. Lovitt, *New German Critique* 16, 1979, 66.

15   For a rich reconstruction, see Stefan Jonsson, *Crowds and Democracy: The Idea and Image of Revolution of the Masses from Revolution to Fascism*, New York: Columbia University Press, 2013.

16   For an account of the genesis, themes, and consequences of Löwenthal and Guterman's study, see my 'Introduction: Psychoanalysis in Reverse', in Leo Löwenthal and Norbert Guterman, *Prophets of Deceit: A Study of the Techniques of the American Agitator*, London: Verso, 2021.

17   Löwenthal and Guterman, *Prophets of Deceit*, 17.

18   Leo Löwenthal, 'Terror's Dehumanizing Effects' (first published in the journal *Commentary* in 1946), in *False Prophets: Studies in Authoritarianism (Communication in Society, Volume 3)*, New York: Routledge, 2017, 183–4.

19   Löwenthal and Guterman, *Prophets of Deceit*, 4, 63, 69.

20   Ibid., 16.

21   Leo Löwenthal, 'Adorno and His Critics', in *Critical Theory and Frankfurt Theorists: Lectures-Correspondence-Conversations (Communication in Society, Vol. 4)*, New Brunswick, NJ: Transaction Publishers, 1989, 51. See also Löwenthal's 'Interview with Helmut Dubiel', in *Critical Theory and Frankfurt Theorists*, 234.

22   Theodor W. Adorno, *The Psychological Technique of Martin Luther Thomas' Radio Addresses*, Stanford: Stanford University Press, 2002, 40–1. (This study, only posthumously published, was Adorno's contribution to the Institute for Social Research's 'agitator project'.) American agitation also had a directly monetisable dimension – as noted in the sub-section on prophets entitled 'The Money-Minded Martyr': 'American agitation is a racket as well as a political movement.' 'Racket' was an important concept for the institute in exile; see Martin Jay, 'Trump, Scorsese, and the Frankfurt School's Theory of Racket Society', *Los Angeles Review of Books*, 5 April 2020.

23   Theodor W. Adorno, 'Freudian Theory and the Pattern of Fascist Propaganda', in *The Frankfurt School Reader*, eds Andrew Arato and Eike Gebhardt, New York: Continuum, 1982, 119.

24   Peter E. Gordon, 'The Authoritarian Personality Revisited: Reading Adorno in the Age of Trump', *b2o*, 15 June 2016.

25   Theodor W. Adorno, 'Remarks on the Authoritarian Personality' (1958), cited in Peter E. Gordon, 'The Authoritarian Personality Revisited: Reading Adorno in the Age of Trump', *b2o*.

26   Adorno, 'Freudian Theory and the Pattern of Fascist Propaganda', 120.

27   Ibid., 123. The National Socialist affirmation of fanaticism, and its circulation as a building-block in Nazi discourse, is forensically explored in Victor Klemperer, 'Fanatical', in *The Language of the Third Reich: LTI – Lingua Tertii Imperii: A Philologist's Notebook*, trans. M. Brady, London: Continuum, 2006, 52–6.

28   Ibid., 126.

29   Ibid., 126–7.

30   Ibid., 132.

31   Ibid., 130.

32   Ibid., 127–8.

33   Ibid., 131.

34   Ibid., 136.

35   Ibid., 136–7.

36   While other commentators have drawn on Sartre's analysis of fused and pledged groups to think through the emergence and action of fascist groupuscules in the present, especially the contemporary avatars of the warrior bands or *Männerbunde* so dear to thinkers of the radical right, Banaji's use of the *Critique* generates a more powerful frame to think of large-scale dynamics of fascisation in the present. For a suggestive study of contemporary *Männerbunde* which draws on Celia Amorós's feminist refunctioning of Sartre, see Jack Z. Bratich, *On Microfascism: Gender, War, and Death*, Brooklyn, NY: Common Notions, 2022, especially chapter 3.

37   Jairus Banaji, 'Trajectories of fascism: Extreme-right movements in India and elsewhere', in *Fascism: Essays on Europe and India*, ed. J. Banaji, Gurgaon: Three Essays Collective, 2013, 223. My emphasis.

38   Alain Badiou, *Infinite Thought: Truth and the Return of Philosophy*, London: Continuum, 2003, 153.

39   Étienne Balibar, 'Racism and Nationalism', in Étienne Balibar and Immanuel Wallerstein, *Race, Nation, Class: Ambiguous Identities*, London: Verso, 1988, 54, 59.

40   On the national-social state, see Étienne Balibar, 'The National Form: History and Ideology', in Balibar and Wallerstein, *Race, Nation, Class*, 137.

41   Leo Lowenthal, 'Letter to Theodor W. Adorno, 13 October 1944', in *Critical Theory and Frankfurt Theorists*, 132.

42   Walter Benjamin, 'The Work of Art in the Age of Its Technological Reproducibility (Second Version)', in *Selected Writings, Volume 3, 1935–1938*, eds Howard Eiland and Michael W. Jennings, Cambridge, MA: Belknap Press, 2002, 129.

43   Andrea Cavalletti, *Class*, ed. Alberto Toscano, trans. Elisa Fiaccadori, Calcutta and London: Seagull Books, 2019, 55.

44   Adorno to Benjamin, 18 March 1936, in Theodor W. Adorno and Walter Benjamin, *The Complete Correspondence, 1928–1940*, ed. Henri Lonitz, trans. Nicholas Walker, Cambridge: Polity Press, 1999, 132–3.

2. Racial Fascism

1   On Toni Morrison's reflections on fascism, see Roderick Ferguson's illuminating essay, 'We Cannot Be the Same After the Siege', *Allies*, eds Ed Pavlić et al., Cambridge, MA: Boston Review, 2019. See also Ferguson's powerful call for an anti-fascist politicisation grounded in queer of colour critique in 'Authoritarianism and the Planetary Mission of Queer of Color Critique', *Safundi: The Journal of South African and American Studies* 21: 3, 2020, 282–90.

2   Mike Baker and Evan Hill, 'Police Say an Antifa Activist Likely Shot at Officers. His Gun Suggests Otherwise', *New York Times*, 10 April 2021.

3   The recent *New York Review of Books* debate featuring Peter E. Gordon, Sam Moyn and Sarah Churchwell provides an informative panorama of positions on this question. Peter E. Gordon, 'Why Historical Analogy Matters', *The New York Review of Books*, 7 January 2020; Samuel Moyn, 'The Trouble with Comparisons', *The New York Review of Books*, 19 May 2020; Sarah Churchwell, 'American Fascism: It Has Happened Here', *The New York Review of Books*, 22 June 2020.

4   Cedric J. Robinson, 'Fascism and the Response of Black Radical Theorists', in *Racial Capitalism, Black Internationalism and Cultures of Resistance*, ed. H. L. T. Quan, London: Pluto, 2019, 149.

5   Quoted in Bill Schwartz, 'George Padmore', in *West Indian Intellectuals in Britain*, ed. Bill Schwartz, Manchester: Manchester University Press, 2003, 141–2. Though unlike Padmore he maintained his fealty to Soviet Communism, R. Palme Dutt also discerned the continuities between European fascism and Empire: 'In the poems of a Kipling, in the Boer

War agitation of a *Daily Mail*, in the war dictatorship of a Lloyd George riding roughshod over constitutional forms and driving to the aim of a "Knock-out Blow", the spirit of Fascism is already present in embryonic forms.' R. Palme Dutt, *Fascism and Social Revolution*, London: Lawrence & Wishart, 1935, 240. See also Alfie Hancox, 'Fasciation as an Expression of imperialist Decay: Rajani Palme Dutt's *Fascism and Social Revolution*', *Liberated Texts*, 23 March 2021.

6   'Every colonial nation carries the seeds of fascist temptation in its bosom. What is fascism, if not a regime of oppression for the benefit of a few?' Albert Memmi, *The Colonizer and the Colonized*, London: Earthscan, 2003 [1957], 106–7; Walter Rodney, *How Europe Underdeveloped Africa*, London: Verso, 2018, 243.

7   Langston Hughes, 'Too Much of Race', *Crisis* 44.9 (September 1937), 272. See also the poem 'Beaumont to Detroit: 1943', whose final lines are: 'How long I got to fight / BOTH HITLER – AND JIM CROW.'

8   I borrow the term 'racial fascism' from Baraka, who crucially posits a violent dialectic between the dynamics of racial domination in the United States and imperialism, a theme that Du Bois himself had powerfully underscored as early as 'The African Roots of War' (1915): 'Andrew Johnson's point position in overthrowing Reconstruction and imposing a racial fascism on Afro America and the Afro American people readied the whole of the U.S. nation for imperialist rule, which today has moved to complete control of the entire nation.' Amiri Baraka, 'Black Reconstruction: Du Bois & the U.S. Struggle for Democracy & Socialism', *Conjunctions* 29, 1997, 78.

9   Harootunian, 'A Fascism for Our Time'. Harootunian details the 'founding oligarchical intentions' and constitutional constructions that, in conjunction with the material histories of racial capitalism, have seeded *sui generis* fascist potentials into the US body politic and its ruling institutions.

10   Jean Genet, 'May Day Speech', in *The Declared Enemy: Texts and Interviews*, trans. Jeff Fort, ed. Albert Dichy, Stanford: Stanford University Press, 2004, 38.

11   On anti-imperialist anti-fascism as coalitional politics among people of colour in the United States, see also the fascinating essay by Michael Staudenmaier, '"America's Scapegoats": Ideas of Fascism in the Construction of the US Latina/o/x Left, 1973-83', *Radical History Review* 138 (special issue on 'Fascism and Anti-fascism since 1945') (October 2020): 39–59.

12   See for instance the dossier on 'new fascism, new democracy', organised by Maoist militants around *La Cause du peuple* in *Les Temps modernes* 310 (1972), especially André Glucksmann's article 'Fascisme: L'ancien et le nouveau'. For the French Trotskyist debate, see Brohm et al., *Le gaullisme, et après? État fort et fascisation*, Paris: François Maspero, 1974. The best critical appraisal of theories of fascism in the US revolutionary left in the 1970s is Noel Ignatin (Ignatiev), 'Fascism: Some Common Misconceptions', *Urgent Tasks* 4 (1978): 1–8.

13   George Jackson, *Blood in My Eye*, London: Penguin, 1975 [1972], 121–2. For a contemporary theoretical discussion of Jackson's theses, see ARM (Association for the Realization of Marxism), 'George Jackson, monopoly capitalism and the fascist type of state', *The Black Liberator* 2: 3, 1974/5.

14   Jean-Paul Sartre, 'A Plea for Intellectuals', in *Between Existentialism and Marxism*, New York: Basic Books, 1974, 256.

15   Jacques Derrida, 'Letter to Jean Genet (fragments)', *Negotiations*, ed. and trans. Elizabeth Rottenberg, Stanford: Stanford University Press, 2002, 43. See also Mikkel Bolt Rasmussen, 'Yes Of Course … Derrida to Genet on Commitment in Favor of Jackson', *New Formations* 75, 2012, 140–53; Tyler M. Williams, 'Derrida and the Censorship of Literature', *The New Centennial Review* 20: 1, 2020, 1–22.

16   Aimé Césaire, *Discourse on Colonialism*, trans. Joan Pinkham, introd. Robin D. G. Kelley, New York: Monthly Review Press, 2001, 36. Where Pinkham translates 'boomerang', the original French speaks of a *choc en retour*, a recoil, return shock or backlash.

17   Mullen and Vials (eds), *The US Antifascism Reader*, 271 (editorial introduction to Penny Nakatsu's speech at the United Front against Fascism Conference, July 1969). See also the discussion of the 'spatial metaphor' of fascism in Christopher Vials, *Haunted by Hitler: Liberals, the Left, and the Fight Against Fascism in the United States*, Amherst: University of Massachusetts Press, 2014, 159–93.

18   Jackson, *Blood in My Eye*, 124, 125.

19   Ibid.

20   Ibid., 126.

21   Theodore W. Allen, *The Invention of the White Race, Volume 2: The Origin of Racial Oppression in Anglo-America*, new ed., introd. Jeffrey B. Perry, London: Verso, 2012.

22   Ibid., 148

23   Ibid., 158. See also Kathleen Cleaver, 'Racism, Fascism, and Political Murder', *The Black Panther*, 14 September 1968, 8.

24   Herbert Marcuse, 'USA: Questions of Organization and the Revolutionary Subject', *The New Left and the 1960s: Collected Papers of Herbert Marcuse, Vol. 3*, ed. Douglas Kellner, London: Routledge, 2005, 138. The notion of preventive counterrevolution had been used to define fascism in the Italian anarchist Luigi Fabbri's *La contro-rivoluzione preventiva. Riflessioni sul fascismo*, Bologna: L. Cappelli, 1922. See also Dutt, *Fascism and Social Revolution*, 123.

25   Étienne Balibar, 'Outlines of a Topography of Cruelty: Citizenship and Civility in the Era of Global Violence', *Constellations* 8: 1, 2001, 16.

26   Marcuse, 'USA', 137–8. The question of fascism's new modalities is a leitmotiv in the writings of Marcuse's last decade. Sometimes he stresses, as in this passage, the objective possibility of a new fascism; at others, he soberly notes the limited if real freedoms that residually obtain in liberal capitalist democracies. See also Herbert Marcuse, 'Le Monde Diplomatique' [1976], in *Marxism, Revolution and Utopia: Collected Papers of Herbert Marcuse, Vol. 6*, eds Douglas Kellner and Clayton Pierce, London: Routledge, 2014, 360.

27   Jackson, *Blood in My Eye*, 162.

28   Angela Y. Davis and Bettina Aptheker, 'Preface', in Angela Y. Davis (ed.), *If They Come in the Morning: Voices of Resistance*, London: Verso, 2016 [1971], xiv. See also Angela Y. Davis, 'Political Prisoners, Prisons and Black Liberation', in *If They Come in the Morning*, 37.

29   Half a century on, Davis insists on the relevance of the category of fascism and its character as a reaction to Black liberation struggles. See 'Interview with Angela Y. Davis', in *Revolutionary Feminisms: Conversations on Collective Action and Radical Thought*, eds Brenna Bhandar and Rafeef Ziadah, London: Verso, 2020, 209–10. Davis's principal reference in her discussion of fascism remains Marcuse, especially his 1934 essay 'The Struggle against Liberalism in the Totalitarian View of the State'.

30   Angela Y. Davis, 'Political Prisoners, Prisons and Black Liberation', in *If They Come in the Morning*, 41.

31   Ibid., 44.

32   Angela Y. Davis and Bettina Aptheker, 'Preface', in *If They Come in the Morning*, xv; Davis, 'Political Prisoners, Prisons and Black Liberation', in *If They Come in the Morning*, 41.

33   Angela Y. Davis, 'Race and Criminalization: Black Americans and the

Punishment Industry', in *The Angela Y. Davis Reader*, ed. Joy James, New York: Blackwell Publishers, 1998, 63. Cited in Dylan Rodriguez, *Forced Passages: Imprisoned Radical Intellectuals and the U.S. Prison Regime*, Minneapolis: University of Minneapolis Press, 2006, 141.

34 Rodriguez, *Forced Passages*, 117.

35 Ibid., 130.

36 Ibid., 137. For a provocative exploration of the superimposition of fascism and liberal legality under late capitalist crisis conditions, see Antonio Negri, 'Fascismo e diritto: un esperimento di metodo', in *Macchina tempo. Rompicapi Liberazione Costituzione*, Milan: Feltrinelli, 1982, 170–92. See also 'Interview with Toni Negri (1980)', in *Revolution Retrieved: Writings on Marx, Keynes, Capitalist Crisis and New Social Subjects (1967–1983)*, London: Red Notes, 1988, 122.

37 Rodriguez, *Forced Passages*, 140–1.

38 'The Afterlife of Fascism', *South Atlantic Quarterly* 105: 1, 2006, 79.

39 Tiago Saraiva, *Fascist Pigs: Technoscientific Organisms and the History of Fascism*, Cambridge, MA: The MIT Press, 138. Saraiva's book is an immensely original and methodologically rich study of fascism in its settler-colonial dimensions, drawing critically on studies of science and technology.

40 Nikhil Pal Singh, *Race and America's Long War*, Berkeley: University of California Press, 2017, 26.

41 Ibid., 172–3. The juridical devices for the dispossession and racialisation of indigenous people in the United States in turn played a formative role in Nazi legal thought, which extended Hitlerism's self-identification as a White settler-colonial project (the *Generalplan Ost* as replica of Manifest Destiny) into racial laws forged after the US example. See James Q. Whitman's enlightening *Hitler's American Model: The United States and the Making of Nazi Race Law*, Princeton: Princeton University Press, 2018.

42 Joshua Myers, *Cedric Robinson: The Time of the Black Radical Tradition*, Cambridge: Polity Press, 2021, 194–5; Cedric J. Robinson, 'Fascism and the Response of Black Radical *Theorists*', in *On Racial Capitalism, Black Internationalism and Cultures of Resistance*, ed. H. L. T. Quan, London: Pluto, 2019, 149. This essay complements Robinson's earlier excavation of the autonomy of Black anti-fascist movements in the context of mobilisations around the invasion of Ethiopia by Fascist Italy: 'Fascism and the Intersections of Capitalism, Racialism, and Historical Consciousness' (1983), in *On Racial Capitalism*, 87–109. On the disjunction between

Third World and Black anti-imperialist anti-fascism and Popular Front anti-fascisms, the key conjuncture of 1935–6, and the repercussions of interwar debates on the 1970s, see Giuliana Chamedes, 'How to Do Things with Words: Antifascism as a Differentially Mobilizing Ideology, from the Popular Front to the Black Power Movement', *Journal of the History of Ideas* 84: 1, 2023, 127–55.

43 Robinson, 'Fascism and the Response of Black Radical *Theorists*', 152.

44 Ibid.

45 Ibid., 155. For a judicious and sympathetic criticism of Robinson's efforts to make the Black radical tradition incongruent with Marxist theory, see Minkah Makalani, *In the Cause of Freedom: Radical Black Internationalism from Harlem to London, 1917–1939*, Chapel Hill: The University of North Carolina Press, 2011, 12–15.

46 Ibid., 156, 157. On the affinities between Césaire's discourse and Robinson's reflections on Black anti-fascism, see Robin D. G. Kelley, 'A Poetics of Anticolonialism', in Césaire, *Discourse on Colonialism*, 20–1. See also Kelley, *Freedom Dreams: The Black Radical Imagination*, Boston: Beacon Press, 2022, 55–7.

47 Ibid.

48 See my '"America's Belgium": W. E. B. Du Bois on Class, Race, and the Origins of World War 1', in *Cataclysm 1914: World War 1 and the Making of Modern World Politics*, ed. Alexander Anievas, Leiden: Brill, 2014.

49 Du Bois speaks of a 'new fascist capitalism' built on the hyper-exploitation of the 'workers of the darker races' in *Black Folk Then and Now: An Essay in the History and Sociology of the Negro Race*, Oxford: Oxford University Press, 2007 [1939], 93. Robinson's passing account of fascism in *Black Marxism* is arguably more precise when it comes to mediating class rule and racial ideology than his essay on Black theorists of fascism. See Cedric J. Robinson, *Black Marxism: The Making of the Black Radical Tradition*, Chapel Hill: The University of North Carolina Press, 2000 [1983], 20–1.

50 There have also been attempts critically to reflect on fascist potentials within Black nationalism broadly construed, from C. L. R. James's observations on Garveyism to Paul Gilroy's suggestion that 'fascism remains latent in any attempt to organize social life according to raciological principles', including in forms of absolutist, militarised or masculinist Black politics. See C. L. R. James, 'Marcus Garvey', in *C. L. R. James on the 'Negro Question'*, ed. Scott McLemee, Jackson: University of Mississipi

Press, 1996, 114–16; Paul Gilroy, 'Black Fascism', *Transition* 81/82, 2000, 70–91.

51   I take this terminology from Devin Zane Shaw's spirited criticism of an earlier version of this argument in *Boston Review*, 'On Toscano's Critique of "Racial Fascism"', *threewayfight*, 30 December 2020.

52   For critical remarks on the limits of the anti-fascist left as well as an account of mass anti-fascist resistance by Black and Asian youth in the British context, see Darcus Howe, 'Enter Mrs Thatcher' (February 1978) and 'The Bradford 12: Reflecting on the Trial of the Decade' (August 1982), in *Here to Stay, Here to Fight: A 'Race Today' Anthology*, eds Paul Field, Robin Bunce, Leila Hassan and Margaret Peacock, London: Pluto, 2019, 23, 159. See also Colin Prescod, 'Black People Against State Harassment (BASH) campaign – a report', *Race & Class* 58: 1, 2016, 96. Prescod's article was originally published in the journal *The Black Liberator* in 1978.

53   Stuart Hall, 'The Great Moving Right Show', *Marxism Today*, January 1979, 15.

54   It is worth noting that the 1970s and early 1980s saw the surge of the 'Third Klan' and a confluence between traditional vehicles for white supremacy and various neo-Nazi formations, which in turn shaped Black radical and far left anti-fascist practice and theory. See Robin D. G. Kelley, 'Foreword' in Hilary Moore and James Tracy, *No Fascist USA! The John Brown Anti-Klan Committee and Lessons for Today's Movements*, San Francisco: City Lights, 2020. For a perspective on how this conjuncture shaped the theorising of fascism in the anti-racist and new communist left, see Ken Lawrence, 'The Ku Klux Klan and Fascism' (1982), in *The US Antifascism Reader*, 289–99, and Paul Saba, 'Fighting Fascism and the Ku Klux Klan', *Viewpoint Magazine*, 10 October 2017.

55   Ruth Wilson Gilmore, 'Terror Austerity Race Gender Excess Theater', in *Abolition Geography: Essays Towards Liberation*, eds Brenna Bhandar and Alberto Toscano, London: Verso, 2022, 161.

56   Ibid., 167; see especially Gilmore, 'Globalisation and U.S. Prison Growth: From Military Keynesianism to Post-Keynesian Militarism', 'Race, Prisons and War: Scenes from the History of US Violence', and 'Prisons and Class Warfare', in *Abolition Geography*.

57   Domenico Losurdo, *Liberalism: A Counter-History*, London: Verso, 2014, 150.

58   Gilmore, *Abolition Geography*, 166.

59   See Shane Burley, 'The Autumn of the Alt Right', *Commune Magazine*, 21
      February 2020. For a forensic chronicle of how white nationalism came to
      be embedded in the US executive, see Michael Edison Hayden, 'Stephen
      Miller's Affinity for White Nationalism Revealed in Leaked Emails',
      Southern Poverty Law Center, 12 November 2019. See also Alexandra
      Minna Stern, *Proud Boys and the White Ethnostate: How the Alt-Right
      is Warping the American Imagination*, Boston: Beacon Press, 2019, ch. 6:
      'Normalizing Nationalism'.

60   Nicos Poulantzas, 'On the Popular Impact of Fascism', in *The Poulantzas
      Reader: Marxism, Law and the State*, ed. James Martin, London: Verso,
      2008, 265. For an excellent presentation of the trajectory and contem-
      porary relevance of Poulantzas's theorising on authoritarianism, see
      Panagiotis Sotiris, 'The Work of Nicos Poulantzas is Vital for Under-
      standing the Authoritarian Right', *Jacobin*, 5 January 2023.

61   David Edgar, 'Racism, Fascism and the Politics of the National Front',
      Race & Class 19: 2, 1977, 112. For Edgar, it remained vital in the late
      1970s and early 1980s to distinguish, politically and analytically, between
      neo-fascist movements and the racist state. See David Edgar, 'The Inter-
      national Face of Fascism' (Speech at the National Anti-Klan Network
      Conference, Atlanta, 19 June 1982), *Urgent Tasks* 14, 1982, 4.

62   Wendy Brown, 'Neoliberalism's Frankenstein: Authoritarian Freedom
      in Twenty-First Century "Democracies"', in Wendy Brown, Peter E.
      Gordon, Max Pensky, *Authoritarianism: Three Inquiries in Critical Theory*,
      Chicago: University of Chicago Press, 2018, 21; see chapter 4 below.

63   Wendy Brown, 'Neoliberalism's Frankenstein', 22.

64   It is also worth noting that within intellectual neoliberal collectives,
      explicitly authoritarian and racist currents were also active. Tracing these
      currents, it becomes possible to see 'right-populist thought as not so much
      a backlash against neoliberalism but the realization of possibilities latent
      within it.' See Quinn Slobodian, 'Anti-'68ers and the Racist-Libertarian
      Alliance: How a Schism among Austrian School Neoliberals Helped
      Spawn the Alt Right', *Cultural Politics* 15: 3, 2019, 374.

65   Vials, *Haunted by Hitler*, 165.

66   Ibid., 161, 192.

67   Jeremy Scahill, 'Scholar Robin D.G. Kelley on How Today's Abolitionist
      Movement Can Fundamentally Change the Country', *The Intercept*, 27
      June 2020.

3. Fascist Freedom

1   On Polanyi's analysis of fascism, see Gareth Dale and Mathieu Desian, 'Fascism', in *Karl Polanyi's Political and Economic Thought: A Critical Guide*, eds Gareth Dale, Christopher Holmes and Maria Markantona-tou, Newcastle upon Tyne: Agenda Publishers, 2019, 151–70. On the wider question of fascism's relation to other expressions of capitalism's congenital 'authoritarian disposition', see Todd Gordon and Jeffery R. Webber, 'The Return of Fascism?', *Spectre*, forthcoming 2023.

2   Soon thereafter, the term would employed pejoratively by Pope Pius XI and critically analysed by Gramsci in his *Prison Notebooks*. See Antonio Gramsci, *Quaderni del carcere*, vol. 2, ed. Valentino Gerratana, Turin: Einaudi, 2007 [1975], 1020–1.

3   Andreas Malm and The Zetkin Collective, *White Skin, Black Fuel: On the Danger of Fossil Fascism*, London: Verso, 2021, 191–2.

4   Ibid., 8.

5   Tyler Stovall, *White Freedom: The Racial History of an Idea*, Princeton, NJ: Princeton University Press, 2021, 214. I explore reactionary and racialised figurations of freedom by contrast with their abolitionist antagonists in Alberto Toscano, 'Freedom', in *Terms of Disorder: Keywords for an Interregnum*, London and Calcutta: Seagull, 2023.

6   Herbert Marcuse, 'Some Social Implications of Modern Technology', in *Technology, War and Fascism: Collected Papers of Herbert Marcuse, Volume 1*, ed. Douglas Kellner, London: Routledge, 1998, 62.

7   Quoted in Christine Vodovar, 'Einaudi e l'avvento del regime fascista', in *Luigi Einaudi. Guida alla lettura. Antologia degli scritti*, 2012, luigieinaudi .it.

8   Giovanni Gentile, *La riforma della scuola in Italia*, Florence: Le Lettere, 1989, 94–5.

9   Quoted in Stovall, *White Freedom*, 214.

10 Benito Mussolini, '[Discorso di Napoli] 24 Ottobre 1922', in Fabio Frosini, *La costruzione dello Stato nuovo. Scritti e discorsi di Benito Mussolini, 1921– 1932*, Venice: Marsilio, 2022, 115.

11 Hugh R. Trevor-Roper and Gerhard L. Weinberg (eds), *Hitler's Table Talk, 1941–1944: Secret Conversations*, New York: Enigma Books, 2008, 10.

12 Robert O. Paxton, *The Anatomy of Fascism*, New York: Alfred A. Knopf, 2004, 90.

13   Salvatore Lupo, *Il fascismo. La politica in un regime totalitario*, Milan: Feltrinelli, 2013, 120.

14   Emilio Gentile, *Fascismo. Storia e interpretazione*, Bari: Laterza, 2002, 16.

15   Curzio Malaparte, *Tecnica del colpo di stato*, in *Opere scelte*, ed. Luigi Marellini, Milan: Arnaldo Mondadori, 1997, 281. Guérin would shortly thereafter write of how 'fascism physically destroys everything opposing its dictatorship, no matter how mildly, and that it creates a vacuum around itself and leaves a vacuum behind it'. This accounts for its bewildering staying power. See Daniel Guérin, *Fascism and Big Business*, New York: Pathfinder, 1973, 370.

16   Ibid., 258.

17   Quoted by Malaparte, *Tenica del colpo di stato*, 287.

18   Mussolini, '[Discorso alla camera dei deputati] 21 Giugno 2021', in *La costruzione dello stato nuovo*, 69.

19   Ibid., 63.

20   Ibid.

21   Ibid., 68.

22   On the eve of the National Fascist Party's foundational congress, the journalist and leading fascist politician Massimo Rocca wrote an article for the journal *Risorgimento* arguing for a 'moderate right' position within the movement, against the Fascist left and the extreme right. Its title was '*Un neo-liberalismo?*' Lupo, *Il fascismo*, 112–13.

23   Mussolini, '[Discorso di Udine] 20 Settembre 1922', in *La costruzione dello Stato nuovo*, 105.

24   Ibid.

25   Mussolini, 'Discorso all'Augusteo – 8 Novembre 2021', in *La costruzione dello Stato nuovo*, 71.

26   Guérin, *Fascism and Big Business*, 155.

27   Franz L. Neumann, *Behemoth: The Structure and Practice of National Socialism, 1933–1944*, Chicago: Ivan R. Dee, 2009 [1944], 467–70. See also Ajay Singh Chaudhary and Raphaële Chappe, 'The Supermanagerial Reich', *LA Review of Books*, 7 November 2016.

28   Johann Chapoutot, *Libres d'obéir. Le management, du nazisme à aujourd'hui*, Paris: Gallimard, 2020. On Chapoutot, see also Marco D'Eramo, 'Rule by Target', *Sidecar – New Left Review*, 15 October 2021. For Hitler's rather narrower rhetorical reference to German freedom as racial-national freedom expressed in the struggle against competitors, see his 9 September 1936 Nuremberg speech, with its nebulous anti-capitalism. Quoted in

Charles Willard Huber, *An Examination of Certain Elements of Rhetorical Style in Nine Selected Speeches of Adolf Hitler*, M.A. Dissertation, Montana State University, 1959, scholarworks.umt.edu, 96–7.

29   Johann Chapoutot, *The Law of Blood: Thinking and Acting as a Nazi*, trans. Miranda Richmond Mouillot, Cambridge, MA: The Belknap Press of Harvard University Press, 2018, 127.

30   Ibid., 34.

31   Johann Chapoutot and Katharina Brienne, 'How the Nazis Pioneered Management Theory' (interview), *Berliner Zeitung*, 16 June 2021. This also resonates with the Orientalist pronouncement of the Nazi jurist Helmut Nicolai: 'Germanic loyalty is the exact antithesis of Eastern obedience' (quoted in Chapoutot, *The Law of Blood*, 183).

32   Chapoutot and Brienne, 'How the Nazis Pioneered Management Theory'.

33   Chapoutot, *The Law of Blood*, 167. In *Eros and Civilization*, Marcuse, no doubt informed by his critical analysis of National Socialism, would treat the performance principle as a key component in the libidinal economy of modern society, one that required systematic dismantling if liberation were to be achieved. On the Nazi ideology of performance and its link to the idea of creative, artistic labour, see Eric Michaud, *The Cult of Art in Nazi Germany*, trans. Janet Lloyd, Stanford: Stanford University Press, 2004.

34   For an illuminating analysis and critique of Arendt's view of totalitarianism as a return-effect of imperialism, and how it reproduces a racialised vision of 'savage' Africa familiar from Conrad's *Heart of Darkness*, see Dorian Bell, *Globalizing Race: Antisemitism and Empire in French and European Culture*, Evanston: Illinois University Press, 2018. See also Samuel Moyn's 2022 Carlyle Lecture on Arendt and 'white freedom', in his *Liberalism Against Itself: Cold War Political Thought and the Making of Our Times*, New Haven: Yale University Press, 2023, and Kathryn T. Gines (now Kathryn Sophia Belle), *Hannah Arendt and the Negro Question*, Bloomington: Indiana University Press, 2014.

35   Hannah Arendt, *The Origins of Totalitarianism*, New York: Harcourt, Brace & Company, 1973 [1951], 404.

36   Ibid., 473; Arendt herself introduces some doubts when she declares, perceptively, that it is 'this freedom from the content of their own ideologies which characterizes the highest rank of the totalitarian hierarchy.' Ibid., 387.

37   Erich Fromm, *Escape from Freedom*, New York: Avon Books, 1969 [1941], 192.

38   Herbert Marcuse, 'State and Individual under National Socialism' [1942], in *Technology, War and Fascism*, 86.

39   Vicky Iakovou, 'Totalitarianism as a Non-State: On Hannah Arendt's Debt to Franz Neumann', *European Journal of Political Theory* 8: 4, 2009, 435; Bernard E. Harcourt, 'Rethinking Capitalism with Franz Neumann, Friedrich Pollock, and the Frankfurt School', *Abolition Democracy*, 17 December 2020, available at blogs.law.columbia.edu.

40   Marcuse, 'State and Individual under National Socialism', 70, 78.

41   Ibid.

42   See especially the 1941 'Research Project on Anti-Semitism', drafted by Adorno, and published in *Studies in Philosophy and Social Science*, now in Theodor W. Adorno, *The Stars Down to Earth: And Other Essays on the Irrational in Culture*, ed. Stephen Crook, London: Routledge, 1994, 181–217; Herbert Marcuse, *Negations: Essays in Critical Theory*, London: Penguin, 1972 [1968], 10.

43   Marcuse, 'State and Individual under National Socialism', 80.

44   For a bracing corrective to the common sense opposition of fascism and liberalism, which delves into the policies advanced by liberal economists after World War I in Italy and the United Kingdom, see Clara E. Mattei, *The Capital Order: How Economists Invented Austerity and Paved the Way to Fascism*, Chicago: University of Chicago Press, 2022.

45   Pierre Dardot, Haud Guéguen, Christian Laval and Pierre Sauvêtre, *Le choix de la guerre civile. Une autre histoire du néolibéralisme*, Montréal: Lux Éditeur, 2021, 292, 293, 21, 49.

46   Ruth Wilson Gilmore, 'Fatal Couplings of Power and Difference: Notes on Racism and Geography', in Gilmore, *Abolition Geography*, 132–53.

47   For further reflections on the anti-state state, see Brenna Bhandar and Alberto Toscano, 'Editors' Introduction: Reports from Occupied Territory', in Gilmore, *Abolition Geography*, 1–22.

48   Ruth Wilson Gilmore and Craig Gilmore, 'Restating the Obvious', in *Abolition Geography*, 262.

49   Gilmore, *Abolition Geography*, 144–5.

50   Ibid., 150–1.

51   Negri, *Revolution Retrieved*, 183.

52   Neoliberal intellectuals' fierce opposition to decolonisation and postcolonial self-determination across the Third World plays a crucial role

in neoliberalism's 'racial constitution'. See Arun Kundnani, 'The Racial Constitution of Neoliberalism', *Race & Class*, 63.1, 2021, 51–69; Robbie Shilliam, 'Enoch Powell: Britain's First Neoliberal Politician', *New Political Economy* 26.2, 2021, 239–49; Lars Cornelissen, 'Neoliberalism and the Racialized Critique of Democracy', *Constellations* 27, 2020, 348–60; Jessica Whyte, *The Morals of the Market: Human Rights and the Rise of Neoliberalism*, London: Verso, 2019; and Slobodian, 'Anti-'68ers and the Racist–Libertarian Alliance'.

53 Stuart Hall, *The Hard Road to Renewal: Thatcherism and the Crisis of the Left*, London: Verso, 1988, 56.

54 Ibid., 71.

55 Ibid., 190, 146.

56 Marcuse, 'State and Individual under National Socialism', 80.

57 Dardot et al., *Le choix de la guerre civile*, 295, 296–7. Neoliberalism's juridical and institutional horizon of constitutionalisation seems largely to have been left behind by those authoritarian libertarians feverishly promoting the accelerated fragmentation of political orders and the evisceration of the last traces of social democracy, or even social liberalism. See Quinn Slobodian, *Crack-Up Capitalism: Market Radical and the Dream of a World Without Democracy*, New York: Metropolitan, 2023. Combining silicone dreams of Caesarist CEOs (Curtis Yarvin) with nationalist white-workerism (J. D. Vance), this festering ideological cluster seems happily to navigate its profound incoherencies and inconsistencies, drawing its unity from that of its putative enemy – a vaporous and insidiously progressive elite 'liberalism' – in endlessly refreshed culture wars. See also James Logue, 'Inside the New Right, where Peter Thiel is placing his biggest bets', *Vanity Fair*, 20 April 2022.

58 Grégoire Chamayou, '1932, la naissance du libéralisme autoritaire', in Carl Schmitt and Hermann Heller, *Du libéralisme autoritaire*, ed. Grégoire Chamayou, Paris: Les Éditions La Découverte/Zones, 2020, 61; see also his *Ungovernable Society: A Genealogy of Authoritarian Liberalism*, trans. Andrew Brown, Cambridge: Polity, 2021.

59 Tony Fitzpatrick quoted in Gilmore, *Abolition Geography*, 279; Ugo Palheta, *La possibilité du fascisme. France, la trajectoire du désastre*, Paris: Les Éditions La Découverte, 2018. See also my review of Palheta's book, 'Trajectories of Fascism', *Historical Materialism* blog, 2021.

60 Karl Polanyi, 'Fascism and Marxian Terminology', *New Britain*, vol. 3, no. 57 (1934), 128.

61 Karl Polanyi, 'The Fascist Virus'.

62 See Cornelissen, 'Neoliberalism and the Racialized Critique of Democracy.'

63 Dale and Desian, 'Fascism', 151. Polanyi employed the term in his 1944 *The Great Transformation.*

64 Malm and Zetkin Collective, *White Skin, Black Fuel*; David E. Lewis, 'Deconstructing the Administrative State', *The Journal of Politics* 81: 3, 2019, 767–89.

4. A Phantom with Limbs of Steel

1 Quoted in Marcuse, *Negations*, 3.

2 Alain Badiou, *The Century*, trans. Alberto Toscano, Cambridge: Polity, 2007, 102.

3 For the debate on 'real abstraction', see my 'The Open Secret of Real Abstraction', in *In the Mind But Not from There: Real Abstraction and Contemporary Art*, ed. Gean Moreno, London: Verso, 2019, 17–41, and the other essays in the collection. I've collected my reflections on this problem in *La abstracción real. Filosofía, estética y capital*, Santiago de Chile: Palinodia, 2021. On romantic anti-capitalism and racial abstraction, see Iyko Day's excellent essay 'The Yellow Plague and Romantic Anticapitalism', *Monthly Review* 72: 3, 2020, 64–73. Day excavates the anti-Asian 'pathogen racism' that courses through the far right's Covid narratives by drawing on Moishe Postone's analysis of the nexus between abstraction and anti-Semitism.

4 Alfred Sohn-Rethel, *The Economy and Class Structure of German Fascism*, trans. Martin Sohn-Rethel, afterword by Jane Caplan, London: Free Association Books, 1987.

5 See Paul Hanebrink, *A Specter Haunting Europe: The Myth of Judeo-Bolshevism*, Cambridge, MA: The Belknap Press of Harvard University Press, 2018.

6 Enzo Traverso, *The Origins of Nazi Violence*, trans. Janet Lloyd, New York: The New Press, 2003, 139.

7 Chapoutot, *The Law of Blood*, 72.

8 Quoted in Ibid., 74. See also Schmitt, 'German Jurisprudence and the Struggle Against the Jewish Spirit', in *The Third Reich Sourcebook*, eds Anson Rabinbach and Sander L. Gilman, Berkeley: University of California Press, 2013, 216–18. It is perhaps not irrelevant here to note how

much these terms repeat Orientalist tropes of the Muslim oscillating between the fanatical abstraction of desert monotheism and the lascivious abandonment of the Harem, or indeed castigations of millenarianism as enthusiasm for the abstract and the frightful admixture of classes and sexes. See my *Fanaticism: On the Uses of an Idea*, London: Verso, 2017, esp. chapter 4.

9   Chapoutot, *The Law of Blood*, 74–5.

10   The quotations from Carl Schmitt in this paragraph are taken from 'National Socialist Legal Thought' (1934), in *The Third Reich Sourcebook*, 134–7.

11   We can register here the imprint of a long lineage of counter-revolutionary polemics: the conjoining of mathematical abstraction and chaotic mixedness in the crucible of revolution is one of the key theses of Edmund Burke, for instance. See my *Fanaticism*, 'Introduction'.

12   Chapoutot, *The Law of Blood*, 78.

13   Ibid., 79.

14   Julius Evola, 'Gli ebrei e la matematica', *La Difesa della razza*, vol. III, n.8, 20 February 1940. On Evola's 'spiritual racism', his opposition to the materialism and empiricism of biological racism and his fierce anti-Semitism, see Francesco Cassata, *'La Difesa della razza'. Politica, ideologia e immagine del razzismo fascista*, Turin: Einaudi, 2008, 76–92, and Francesco Germinario's acute and informative study *Razza del Sangue, razza dello Spirito. Julius Evola, l'antisemitismo e il nazionalsocialismo (1930–1943)*, Turin: Bollati Boringhieri, 2001.

15   Another Institute member, Franz Neumann, would go on to serve as Chief of Research for the prosecution at the Nuremberg trials, in the context of which Schmitt would be interrogated by a friend and colleague of Neumann. See Michael Salter, 'Neo-Fascist Legal Theory on Trial: An Interpretation of Carl Schmitt's Defence at Nuremberg from the Perspective of Franz Neumann's Critical Theory of Law', *Res Publica* 5 (1999): 161–94.

16   'Research Project on Anti-Semitism', in Theodor W. Adorno, *The Stars Down to Earth*, 205. As Franz Neumann noted in *Behemoth*, around the same time, 'Jews occupying primarily intermediary positions were, so to speak, the concrete manifestation of capitalism for the old and new middle classes ... The average German did not and could not see that the Jewish middlemen were, in fact, merely middlemen – representatives of an anonymous power that dictated their economic activities' (122–3).

17 Ibid., 207.

18 For an important reflection on the historical limitations of a view of European Jews as a 'people-class' racially ascribed to intermediary and circulatory functions within capitalism, see Maxime Rodinson's commentary on Abraham Leon's classic work *La conception matérialiste de la question juive* (translated as *The Jewish Question: A Marxist Interpretation*): 'From the Jewish Nation to the Jewish Problem', in Maxime Rodinson, *Cult, Ghetto, and State: The Persistence of the Jewish Question*, London: Al Saqi Books, 1983, 68–117.

19 Ibid., 207–8. See also Mladen Dolar's incisive remarks on racism in general, and anti-Semitism in particular, as constituting not only a 'gigantic displacement' but also a 'gigantic condensation' of class struggle, as evidenced by the fantastical coexistence of (bourgeois) abstraction and (proletarian) abjection in racist images of Jews. Mladen Dolar, 'A proposito del fascismo', in *Il politico e l'inconscio*, eds Viktor Fainberg, Rastko Močnik and Armando Verdiglione, Venice: Marsilio, 1978, 66–7.

20 The 'Research Project' is in this sense aligned with the Pollock-Horkheimer thesis of state or authoritarian capitalism, by contrast with the minority view in the Institute, namely Neumann and Marcuse's, which we explored in our chapter on 'Fascist Freedom'. For Neumann and Marcuse, Nazism had not transcended the ambit of competitive capitalism or generated a durable fusion of economy and the state under the primacy of the latter.

21 Ibid., 211–13.

22 See Lucio Colletti's 'Introduction' to Karl Marx, *Early Writings*, London: Penguin, 1975, for important insights on the way 'On the Jewish Question' and other contemporaneous writings by Marx delineate the problem of real abstraction across the demarcation between the political and the economic.

23 Theodor Adorno, Else Frenkel-Brunswik, Daniel J. Levinson, and R. Nevitt Sanford, *The Authoritarian Personality*, introd. Peter E. Gordon, London: Verso, 2019, lxiii. There is a remarkable anticipation of this thesis in Adorno's 1941 essay on Oswald Spengler. Theodor W. Adorno, 'Spengler Today', *Studies in Philosophy and Social Science* IX (1941), 308.

24 See Alberto Toscano and Jeff Kinkle, *Cartographies of the Absolute*, Winchester: Zero Books, 2015.

25 Adorno et al., *The Authoritarian Personality*, 665.

26 Ibid.

27   Ibid., 666. See also Gillian Rose's astute critical remarks on the question of stereotypy and reification in Adorno in Gillian Rose, *The Melancholy Science: An Introduction to the Thought of Theodor W. Adorno*, London: Verso, 2014, 108.

28   This dimension was explored by Moishe Postone, as noted by Neil Levi in his excellent critical study 'Power, Politics, and Personification: Toward a Critique of Postone's Theory of Antisemitism', forthcoming in the journal *Historical Materialism*.

29   For a wide-ranging and insightful 'updating' of *The Authoritarian Personality* in light of contemporary networked digital communication and its impact on political behaviours, see Moira Weigel, 'The Authoritarian Personality 2.0', *Polity* 54: 1, 2022, 146–80; see also Jessie Daniels, 'The Algorithmic Rise of the "Alt-Right"', *Contexts* 17: 1, 2018, 60–5.

30   Theodor W. Adorno, *Guilt and Defense: On the Legacies of National Socialism in Postwar Germany*, eds Jeffrey K. Olick and Andrew J. Perrin, Cambridge, MA: Harvard University Press, 2010; Friedrich Pollock, Theodor W. Adorno and collaborators, *Group Experiment and Other Writings: The Frankfurt School on Public Opinion in Postwar Germany*, eds Jeffrey K. Olick and Andrew J. Perrin, Cambridge, MA: Harvard University Press, 2011.

31   Theodor W. Adorno, 'The Meaning of Working Through the Past', in *Critical Models: Interventions and Catchwords*, trans. Henry W. Pickford, introd. Lydia Goehr, New York, NY: Columbia University Press, 2005, 90.

32   Ibid., 344.

33   Ibid., 98–9. See also my discussion in chapter 1 of Adorno's 1951 essay on Freudian theory and fascism.

34   Theodor W. Adorno, *Aspects of the New Right-Wing Extremism*, trans. Wieland Hoban, Cambridge: Polity, 2020.

35   Guterman was himself on the margins of the Institute, and Lefebvre penned a review for the Institute's *Zeitschrift*. Whether and how they would have come across the ideas of Sohn-Rethel is a matter for some future detective work.

36   Norbert Guterman and Henri Lefebvre, *La conscience mystifiée. Suivi de Henri Lefebvre, La Conscience privée*, Paris: Syllepse, 1999, 176.

37   See my 'Observations on Capitalist Folklore', *Viewpoint Magazine*, 24 April 2019.

38   Ibid., 180.

39   Ibid., 181.
40   Ibid., 140.
41   Ibid., 173.
42   Ibid., 170.
43   See especially Jean-Joseph Goux, *Symbolic Economies: After Marx and Freud*, trans. Jennifer Curtiss Gage, Ithaca: Cornell University Press, 1990, and Marc Shell, *Money, Language, Thought: Literary and Philosophic Economies from the Mediaeval to the Modern*, Baltimore: Johns Hopkins University Press, 1993.
44   Guterman and Lefebvre, *La Conscience mystifiée*, 92.
45   Ibid., 108.
46   Ibid., 137, 171.
47   Ibid., 157.
48   Ibid., 163.
49   Ibid., 141.

5. Rushing Forward Into the Past

1   Karl Polanyi, 'The Fascist Virus', n.d. [draft manuscript from the 1930s], kpolanyi.scoolaid.net:8080/xmlui/handle/10694/658; Harry Harootunian, 'The Future of Fascism', *Radical Philosophy* 136, 2006, 32.
2   Harry Harootunian, 'A Fascism for Our Time', *The Massachusetts Review*, 6 January 2021, massreview.org. On Levi's understanding of fascism and its afterlives, see my afterword to the graphic novel by Matteo Mastragostino and Alessandro Ranghiasci, *Primo Levi*, trans. A. Toscano, Toronto: Between the Lines Books, 2021.
3   Geoff Eley, 'What is Fascism and Where Does it Come From?', *History Workshop Journal* 91, 2021, 6, 1, 15–16.
4   Ibid., 8.
5   Ibid., 7, 15–19; see also Geoff Eley, 'What Produces Fascism: Preindustrial Traditions or a Crisis of a Capitalist State', *Politics & Society* 12: 1, 1983, 53–82.
6   Reinhart Koselleck, 'Crisis', *Journal of the History of Ideas* 67: 2, 2006, 361; Reinhart Koselleck, 'Some Questions Regarding the Conceptual History of "Crisis"', in *The Practice of Conceptual History: Timing History, Spacing Concepts*, trans. Todd Presner, Kerstin Behnke, and Jobst Welge, Stanford: Stanford University Press, 2002, 244.
7   According to Roger Griffin, the 'affective heart of generic fascism was

animated by the sense that a seismic, elemental process of ultranationalist palingenesis was taking place, sweeping away decadence forever, so that fascists felt they were standing on the threshold of a new era, witnessing a new dawn out of which would emerge a new man (accompanied by a new fascist woman), a new or revitalised empire, a new civilisation to regenerate the nation, the race, or even the West in its entirety'. Roger Griffin, 'Fixing Solutions: Fascist Temporalities as Remedies for Liquid Modernity', *Journal of Modern European History* 13: 1, 2015, 17; see also, in the same issue, Claudio Fogu, 'The Fascist Stylisation of Time', 98–114.

8   Harootunian, 'The Future of Fascism', 25.

9   Henri Lefebvre, *Le nationalisme contre les nations*, ed. Michel Trebitsch, Paris: Méridiens-Klincksieck, 1988, 154.

10 Ibid., 155.

11 Ibid., 157.

12 Peter Osborne, *The Politics of Time: Modernity and Avant-Garde*, London: Verso, 1995, 164–5.

13 Griffin, 'Fixing Solutions', 15 and 16. Griffin's suggestion is worth heeding: 'some scholarly effort could be usefully expended on analysing more precisely the relationship between the popular appeal (or lack of it) of the particular myths of rebirth and eternity at the heart of each fascist project and the specific temporal crisis each nation was undergoing in the inter-war period' (21). See also Roger Griffin, *Modernism and Fascism: The Sense of a Beginning under Mussolini and Hitler*, Basingstoke: Palgrave, 2007.

14 Osborne, *The Politics of Time*, 163.

15 Ibid., 167.

16 Ibid., 169.

17 Karl Löwith, 'The Political Implications of Heidegger's Existentialism' [1946], in *The Heidegger Controversy: A Critical Reader*, ed. Richard Wolin, New York: Columbia University Press, 1991.

18 Osborne, *The Politics of Time*, 172–3.

19 Martin Heidegger, *Heraclitus: The Inception of Occidental Thinking and Logic: Heraclitus's Doctrine of the Logos*, trans. Julia Goesser Assaiante and S. Montgomery Ewegen, London: Bloomsbury, 2018, 135. *Beyng* is an archaic spelling for *being*, like *Seyn*, with which the later Heidegger replaced *Sein*.

20 For clarification of the terminology, see Jan Slaby, 'Ontic (*Ontisch*)', in *The Cambridge Heidegger Lexicon*, ed. Mark A. Wrathall, Cambridge:

Cambridge University Press, 2021, 542: 'The ontic concerns concrete properties and characteristics of an entity, in contrast to the ontological which pertains to the specific way an entity of a certain kind has its characteristics. The early to mid Heidegger centrally distinguishes between the ontic (*ontisch*) and the ontological (*ontologisch*), as his foundational move is to keep entities (*Seiendes*) conceptually distinct from being (*Sein*).' William H. F. Altman, *Martin Heidegger and the First World War: Being and Time as Funeral Oration*, Lanham: Lexington Books, 2012.

21 Martin Heidegger, 'The Reunion Speech', in Altman, *Martin Heidegger and the First World War*, 288.

22 There are interesting resonances between Heidegger's reunion speech and Carl Schmitt's 1934 article exalting Hitler's juridical supremacy in the wake the Night of Long Knives. See Carl Schmitt, 'The Führer Protects the Law: On Adolf Hitler's Reichstag Address of 13 July 1934', in *The Third Reich Sourcebook*, 64, 66.

23 Altman, *Martin Heidegger and the First World War*, 288.

24 Heidegger, 'The Reunion Speech', 290.

25 See Domenico Losurdo, *Heidegger and the Ideology of War: Community, Death, and the West*, trans. Marella and Jon Morris, Amherst, NY: Humanity Books, 2001.

26 Quoted in Altman, *Martin Heidegger and the First World War*, 186–7.

27 Altman, *Martin Heidegger and the First World War*, 192–3.

28 Griffin, 'Fixing Solutions', 18.

29 Pierre Bourdieu, *The Political Ontology of Martin Heidegger*, trans. Peter Collier, Stanford: Stanford University Press, 1991, 62–3.

30 Osborne, *The Politics of Time*, 174. Consider also the Vietnamese philosopher Trân Đuc Thao's caustic observation: 'In the decomposition of bourgeois society that had been caused by the ruthlessness of imperialist monopoly, the motto "freedom-towards-death" was offered to the ruined petite bourgeoisie as the final justification of their position as petite-bourgeoisie'. *Phenomenology and Dialectical Materialism*, trans. Daniel J. Hennan and Donald V. Morano, ed. Robert S. Cohen, Dordrecht: D. Reidel, 1986 [1951], xxviii.

31 Kojin Karatani, 'On *The Eighteenth Brumaire of Louis Bonaparte*', in *History and Repetition*, ed. Seiji M. Lippett, New York: Columbia University Press, 2004, 2. See also 'Buddhism and Fascism', in the same volume.

32 Karatani, 'On *The Eighteenth Brumaire of Louis Bonaparte*', 15.

33   Ibid., 16, 10.

34   On the fascist style of 'making history', see Fogu's 'The Fascist Stylisa-
     tion of Time'. Fogu quotes this remarkable 1929 retort by Mussolini
     to Benedetto Croce's criticism of the Concordat with the Vatican: 'No
     wonder, gentlemen, if side by side the shirkers of war we find *the shirkers
     of history*, who, having failed – for many reasons and maybe because of
     their creative impotence – to produce the event, that is, to make history
     before writing it, later on consume their revenge diminishing it without
     objectivity or shame' (my emphasis). Contrast Mussolini's voluntarism
     with Hitler's fate-drenched vision, from a 1933 campaign speech: 'It is
     ultimately a matter of indifference what percentage of the German people
     make history. The only thing that matters is that it is we who are the last
     to make history in Germany'. Quoted in Reinhart Koselleck, *Futures
     Past: On the Semantics of Historical Time*, trans. and introd. Keith Tribe,
     New York: Columbia University Press, 2004, 203.

35   Harootunian, 'Fascism for Our Time', 27.

36   See my 'Capitalism without Capitalism. Fascism According to Žižek',
     Res Pública. Revista de Historia de las Ideas Políticas 23: 3, 2020, 365–73.

37   See Peter Trawny, *Heidegger & the Myth of a Jewish World Conspiracy*,
     trans. Andrew J. Mitchell, Chicago: University of Chicago Press, 2015.

38   Harootunian, 'The Future of Fascism', 28.

39   Mosse, *The Fascist Revolution*, 36.

40   Benito Mussolini, 'Relativismo e fascismo', *Il Popolo d'Italia* 279, 22
     November 1921, 8.

41   Roberto Schwarz, 'Neo-Backwardness in Bolsonaro's Brazil', *New Left
     Review* 123, 2020, 25–38.

42   For an interesting research hypothesis that draws on Lacanian psychoa-
     nalysis to account for this superstructural excess, see Dolar, 'A proposito
     del fascismo'. Dolar suggests that 'fascism is the form of social repro-
     duction in which the survival and affirmation of the *social dominance
     of monopolistic capital* is made possible by the promise of an *imaginary
     dominance in the field of the mechanisms of the signifier*' (69).

43   While I recognise that 'gender ideology' is a reactionary construction and
     meme, in contrast to critical race theory which is a tradition of emancipa-
     tory scholarly work, I write 'critical race theory' in quotation marks to
     signal its confection by the US far right as a conspiratorial bogeyman, to
     be removed by force of legislation from all levels of the education system.

44   Mikkel Bolt Rasmussen, *Late Capitalist Fascism*, Cambridge: Polity, 2022.

45　Fredric Jameson, *Fables of Aggression: Wyndham Lewis, the Modernist as Fascist*, London: Verso, 2008 [1979], 15.

46　Ibid.

47　Ibid.

48　George L. Mosse, *The Fascist Revolution: Toward a General Theory of Fascism*, Madison: The University of Wisconsin Press, 2021 [1999], 110. Consider also Koselleck's pointed reflections on Hitler's penchant for 'self-ultimata' as defining a Nazi politics 'made under the compulsion of an acceleration which stood in an inverse relation to the spaces of time and to the eternity in whose name he claimed to act'. Koselleck, *Futures Past*, 203.

6. Ideas Without Words

1　Three of his books have been translated to date: Furio Jesi, *Spartakus*, introd. Andrea Cavalletti, trans. Alberto Toscano, Calcutta: Seagull, 2013; *Secret Germany: Myth in Twentieth-Century German Culture*, introd. Andrea Cavalletti, trans. Richard Braude, Calcutta: Seagull, 2021; and *Time and Festivity: Essays on Myth and Literature*, ed. Andrea Cavalletti, trans. Cristina Viti, Calcutta: Seagull, 2021. See also the special issue of *Theory & Event* dedicated to Jesi's work: *Theory & Event* 22: 4, 2019.

2　On Evola, Freda and the theories of the post-war radical right in Italy, see Francesco Germinario, *Tradizione, mito, storia. La cultura politica della destra radicale e i suoi teorici*, Rome: Edizioni Carocci, 2014.

3　Furio Jesi, *Cultura di destra. Con tre inediti e un'intervista*, ed. Andrea Cavalletti, Rome: Nottetempo, 2011. 287. On Jesi and right-wing culture, see also Andrea Cavalletti, 'Demolish Right Wing Culture', *Ill Will*, 2 June 2021; Enrico Manera, Wu Ming 1 and Giuliano Santoro, 'Il più odiato dai fascisti. Conversazione su Furio Jesi', *Giap*, 15 January 2013, wumingfoundation.com; Enrico Manera, 'Myth and Right-wing Culture in Furio Jesi', *Theory & Event* 22: 4, 2019, 1069–81; Kieran Aarons, 'Gene-alogy of Far-Right Accelerationism', in *Pólemos. Materiali di filosofia e critica sociale 1/2022 – Furio Jesi: Mitopolitica*, eds Emanuele E. Pelilli and James R. Martel, Rome: Donzelli, 2023, 261–94.

4　Oswald Spengler, *The Hour of Decision, Part I: Germany and World-Historical Revolution*, trans. Charles Francis Atkinson, London: George Allen & Unwin, 1934, xiii. The original reads: '*Was wir von unseren Vätern her im Blute haben, Ideen ohne Worte, ist allein das, was der Zukunft*

Beständigkeit verspricht.' Spengler's book can now be found in print with Rogue Scholars Press, purveyor of sundry texts by Mishima, Céline, Jünger and more current and degraded fare, like the pseudo-Nietzschean provocateur 'Bronze Age Pervert'.

5   Jesi, *Cultura di destra*, 25.

6   Ibid. Ferraresi quotes Hermann Hesse's 1928 *Steppenwolf*, musing that German intellectuals 'are all dreaming of a speech without words that utters the inexpressive and gives form to the formless'. Franco Ferraresi, *Threats to Democracy: The Radical Right in Italy After the War*, Princeton: Princeton University Press, 1992, 261n1. On the Nazi desire to purify language to draw out the 'images beneath the words', see Michaud, *The Cult of Art in Nazi Germany*, 171. For a diagnosis of fascism as the reign of words without ideas, a 'factory of the void', see Franco Venturi, 'Il regime fascista', in *Trent'anni di storia italiana (1915–1945). Lezioni con testimonianze presentate da Franco Antonicelli*, Turin: Einaudi, 1961.

7   Jesi, *Cultura di destra*, 26.

8   Ibid., 28. In an interview around his edition of Spengler's *Decline*, Jesi would observe that the mythological machine functions just as well on the left and the right, 'and with the same rhythm.' However, the right has exercised far less self-censorship in this domain, thereby giving rise to 'an extremely varied and articulated set of exhibitions, reflections and manipulations; a complex of testimonies, deeper and more differentiated than those which can be found on the "left", regarding the functioning of the mythological machine.' Furio Jesi, 'Microscopio e binocolo sulla cultura di destra. Furio Jesi sul libro di Spengler', *L'Ora* (Palermo), 7 September 1978.

9   Furio Jesi, 'Introduzione', in Oswald Spengler, *Il Tramonto dell'Occidente. Lineamenti di una morfologia della storia mondiale*, eds Rita Calabrese Conte, Margherita Cottone and Furio Jesi, introd. Furio Jesi, trans. Julius Evola, Milan: Longanesi & C., 1978, xviii.

10 On Bachofen, see also Furio Jesi, *Mito*, Milan: ISEDI, 1973 (repr. Turin: Aragno, 2008), and *Bachofen*, ed. Andrea Cavalletti, Turin: Bollati Boringhieri, 2005.

11 Jesi, 'Introduzione', in *Il Tramonto dell'Occidente*, xxv.

12 Ibid., xxv.

13 Ibid., xxxi.

14 Oswald Spengler, *Man and Technics: A Contribution to a Philosophy of*

Life, trans. Charles Francis Atkinson, London: George Allen & Unwin, 1931, 104.

15 Cesare Pavese, *Il Taccuino segreto*, ed. Francesca Belviso, Turin: Nino Aragno, 2020. Pavese's secret notebook was first published by the Turin newspaper *La Stampa* on 8 August 1990, causing much controversy and consternation in the Italian cultural left.

16 Jesi, *Cultura di destra*, 159.

17 Furio Jesi, *Letteratura e mito*, Turin: Einaudi, 1968; new ed. with introd. Andrea Cavalletti, Turin: Einaudi, 2002, 175.

18 Ibid., 166.

19 Jesi, *Cultura di destra*, 91, 97, 93. There are interesting resonances between Jesi's account and Jack Bratich's study of the 'homi-suicidal' dimension of contemporary far-right culture in Bratich, *On Microfascism*.

20 Ibid., 91.

21 See the 6 June 1979 entry in Mircea Eliade, *Journal, IV: 1979–1985*, trans. Mac Linscott Ricketts, Chicago: University of Chicago Press, 2018; for Jesi's work on Eliade, see Mircea Eliade, *Lo yoga. Immortalità e libertà*, ed. Furio Jesi, trans. Giorgio Pagliaro, Milan: Rizzoli, 1973. For insights into an ongoing debate on Eliade and fascism, see Philip Ó Ceallaigh, Bryan Rennie, 'Mircea Eliade and Anti-Semitism', *Los Angeles Review of Books*, 13 September 2018; also Mark Weitzman, '"One Knows the Tree by the Fruit That It Bears:" Mircea Eliade's Influence on Current Far-Right Ideology', *Religions* 11, 2020, mdpi.com.

22 Mircea Eliade, 'Master Manole and the Monastery of Arges', in *Zalmoxis, The Vanishing God*, trans. Willard R. Trask, Chicago: University of Chicago Press, 1972, 183–4.

23 Jesi, *Cultura di destra*, 73.

24 Ibid., 74.

25 Ibid., 136.

26 One of the speeches was public, the other delivered in Chirone's freemason lodge, thus neatly spanning the esoteric and the exoteric. As Ingrid Rowland notes, Bruno Jesi, Furio's Jewish father, had been granted Aryan status on the grounds of his military service as a cavalry officer in the invasion of Ethiopia and had died in 1943 of wounds incurred in combat. Notwithstanding the autobiographical dimensions of *Cultura*, especially in its attention to Jewish Fascist milieus and to the linguistic habitus of the Turin bourgeoisie from whence Jesi hailed, the colonial dimension of fascism remains largely unaddressed. See Ingrid D. Rowland, 'Furio Jesi

and the Culture of the Right', in *History of the Humanities III: The Modern Humanities*, eds Rens Bod, Jaap Maat, and Thijs Weststeijn, Amsterdam: Amsterdam University Press, 2014, 293–310.

27   Jesi, *Cultura di destra*, 213.

28   Ibid., 157.

29   Jesi drew repeatedly on Kerényi's idea of 'technicized myth' while abandoning the notion of a genuine myth as counterpart. See Károly Kerényi, 'Dal mito genuino al mito tecnicizzato', in *Tecnica e casistica: tecnica, escatologia e casistica (Colloquio di Roma, 7–12 gennaio 1964)*, ed. Enrico Castelli, Rome: CEDAM, 1964, 153–68.

30   Jesi, *Cultura di destra*, 164.

31   Ibid., 166.

32   Ibid., 165.

33   Ibid., 208.

34   Ibid., 211.

35   Ibid., 218.

36   See Bratich, *On Microfascism*.

37   Spengler had written to Korherr in 1926 that 'up to now I have read nothing which has completed and deepened a suggestion in my book into such knowledge and understanding.' Oswald Spengler, *Letters: 1913–1936*, ed. and trans. Arthur Helps, London: George Allen & Unwin, 1966, 203. See also Richard Korherr, *Regresso delle nascite: morte dei popoli*, pref. Oswald Spengler and Benito Mussolini, Roma: Libreria del Littorio, 1928. On Mussolini's 'obsessional-demographic *Weltanschauung*', see the acerbic reflections in Maria Antonietta Macciocchi, *La donna 'nera.' 'Consenso' femminile e fascismo*, Milan: Feltrinelli, 1976, 75–82.

38   That said, Spengler deemed the Ethiopian war an 'evil adventure' (*Letters*, 305). On the influence of Spengler's conception of Caesarism on Mussolini, see Renzo De Felice, *Mussolini il duce. 1. Gli anni del consenso. 1929–1936*, Turin: Einaudi, 1974.

39   See Chetan Bhatt, 'White Extinction: Metaphysical Elements of Contemporary Western Fascism', *Theory, Culture & Society* 20: 1, 2021, 27–52.

40   I have not been able to find any record of this event.

41   Johann Chapoutot, *Greeks, Romans, Germans: How the Nazis Usurped Europe's Classical Past*, trans. Richard R. Nybakken, Oakland: University of California Press, 2016, 325–6.

7. Cathedrals of Erotic Misery

1 'One section, now lost, in [avant-garde artist Kurt Schwitters's] Hanover Merzbau was called "The Cathedral of Erotic Misery", a rickety monument that contained, secreted in its various "grottos", little mementos solicited or stolen from friends such as Hannah Höch, as well as "a small round bottle with my urine" and pictures of public figures including Hindenburg and Mussolini.' Hal Foster, 'Anyone can do collage', *London Review of Books*, 10 March 2022.

2 Quoted in Chapoutot, *The Law of Blood*, 230.

3 See Judith Butler, 'Why is the idea of "gender" provoking backlash the world over?', *The Guardian*, 23 October 2021.

4 Michel Foucault, 'Schizo-Culture: On Prisons and Psychiatry', in *Foucault Live: Collected Interviews, 1961-1984*, ed. Sylvère Lotringer, trans. Lysa Hochroth and John Johnston, New York: Semiotext(e), 1996 [1989], 179. In a different context, Foucault also reflected on how in the absence of the 'gigantic shadows of fascism and Stalinism' and the 'political anxiety' they induce regarding contemporary societies, his own investigations into the interstices of power would not have assumed the 'direction and intensity' they took on. See Foucault, 'The End of the Monarchy of Sex', in *Foucault Live*, 221.

5 See Alberto Toscano, 'The Intolerable-Inquiry: The Documents of the Groupe d'information sur les prisons', *Viewpoint Magazine*, 25 September 2013.

6 Ibid., 169, 174.

7 Foucault, 'Sade: Sergeant of Sex', in *Foucault Live*, 188. Foucault's dismissal of an erotic framing of Nazism largely resonates with Primo Levi's observations about Nazisploitation cinema in a 1977 newspaper article. See Primo Levi, 'Movies and Swastikas', in *The Complete Works of Primo Levi*, ed. Ann Goldstein, Liverlight: New York, 2015.

8 Foucault, *Foucault Live*, 189.

9 Ibid.

10 Jordy Rosenberg, 'The Daddy Dialectic', *Los Angeles Review of Books*, 11 March 2018.

11 Foucault, 'Preface', in Gilles Deleuze and Félix Guattari, *Anti-Oedipus: Capitalism and Schizophrenia*, trans. Robert Hurley et al., New York: Viking, 1977, xiii.

12 Though emerging out of the same ideological conjuncture, this effort

reflexively to explore an everyday or microfascism should be distinguished from the discourse of 'left fascism' (*Linksfaschismus*) voiced by the likes of Jürgen Habermas in response to radical and armed movements of the 1970s.

13   Quoted in Robin D. G. Kelley, *Freedom Dreams*, 147.

14   Félix Guattari, 'I Am an Idea Thief', in *Soft Subversions: Texts and Interviews, 1977–1985*, ed. Sylvère Lotringer, trans. Chet Wiener and Emily Wittman, introd. Charles J. Stivale, New York: Semiotext(e), 2009, 31. For an earlier version of this same argument, see Guattari, 'Desire is Power, Power is Desire: Answers to the Schizo-Culture Conference', in *Chaosophy: Texts and Interviews, 1972–1977*, ed. Sylvère Lotringer, trans. David L. Sweet, Jarred Becker, and Taylor Adkins, introd. François Dosse, New York: Semiotext(e), 2009, 287. Guattari saw this micropolitical perspective on fascism anticipated by Daniel Guérin's observation that German and Italian interwar capitalism did not wish to 'deprive itself of this incomparable, irreplaceable means of penetrating into all the cells of society, the organization of the fascist masses.' Quoted in Guattari, 'Everybody Wants to be a Fascist', in *Chaosophy*, 165.

15   Guattari, 'A Liberation of Desire', in *Soft Subversions*, 152.

16   Guattari, 'Everybody Wants to be a Fascist', in *Chaosophy*, 164.

17   Ibid., 171. 'A micropolitics of desire means that henceforth we will refuse to allow any fascist formula to slip by, on whatever scale it may manifest itself, including within the scale of the family or even within the scale of our own personal economy' (166).

18   Gilles Deleuze and Michel Foucault, 'Intellectuals and Power', in *Foucault Live*, 80.

19   Foucault, 'Film and Popular Memory', in *Foucault Live*, 127, 129. Foucault's observations can be usefully contrasted with the position taken on the sexualisation of Nazism by Susan Sontag's roughly contemporaneous 'Fascinating Fascism', *New York Review of Books*, 6 February 1975.

20   Ibid., 128.

21   Ibid., 128–9.

22   Guattari, 'Everybody Wants to be a Fascist', 168. Guattari also maps the 'mutation of a new desiring machinism in the masses' onto the specifics of its investment in Hitler's 'style', which combine plebeian and war-veteran elements, with a 'shopkeeper's flexibility' in negotiating with big business and a 'racist delirium' capable of capturing 'the collective death instinct released from the charnel houses of the First World War' (165–6).

23 See the incisive commentary on Theweleit's project in Barbara Ehrenreich's 'Foreword' to Klaus Theweleit, *Male Fantasies, vol. 1 – Women Floods Bodies History*, trans. Stephen Conway with Erica Carter and Chris Turner, Minneapolis: University of Minnesota Press, 1987, ix–xvii. For a striking effort to employ Theweleit's method, see Jonathan Littell's archival essay on the Belgian fascist Léon Degrelle, *Le sec et l'humide. Une brève incursion en territoire fasciste*, Paris: Gallimard, 2008. Littell perceptively notes, following Theweleit, that for the fascist, metaphor (like the feminised communist 'flood') 'is never *only* a metaphor (whence the incredible efficacy of fascist metaphors)' (29).

24 For a brilliant early exploration of the German genealogy of male associations and their role in the germination of Völkisch and Nazi politics, see Hans Mayer, 'The Rituals of Political Association in Germany of the Romantic Period', in *The College of Sociology (1937–1939)*, ed. Denis Hollier, trans. Betsy Wing, Minneapolis: University of Minnesota Press, 1988, 262–78. On the *Bund*-form in the pre-Nazi German nationalist right, see also George L. Mosse, *The Crisis of German Ideology: Intellectual Origins of the Third Reich*, New York: Grosset & Dunlap, 1964, 204–17. It is at the level of the nexus between libido and the organisation of political groups, rather than at a purely psychoanalytic one, that the vexed question of fascism's attraction for certain homosexual intellectuals and elites – notwithstanding its violent homophobia – is best addressed. See for example, George L. Mosse, 'On Homosexuality and French Fascism', in *The Fascist Revolution: Toward a General Theory of Fascism*, Madison: University of Wisconsin Press, 2022, 139–44. On the limited capacity of critical theories of fascism to contend with homosexuality and queerness, see Bruce Baum, 'Queering Critical Theory: Re-Visiting the Early Frankfurt School on Homosexuality and Critique', *Berlin Journal of Critical Theory* 5: 2, 2021, 5–67.

25 Bratich, *On Microfascism*, 52. See also Anson Rabinbach and Jessica Benjamin, 'Foreword', Klaus Theweleit, *Male Fantasies, vol. 2 – Male Bodies: Psychoanalyzing the White Terror*, trans. Erica Carter and Chris Turner with Stephen Conway, Minneapolis: University of Minnesota Press, 1989 xvii. As Rabinbach and Benjamin note: 'Theweleit is not interested in "ideology" as a representation of reality, but in the symbolic construction of the other as a mechanism of self-cohesion' (xxii).

26 Bratich, *On Microfascism*, 30.

27 The proceedings of the seminar are collected in two volumes as *Eléments*

pour une analyse du fascisme. Séminaire de Maria-A. Macciocchi: Paris VIII – Vincennes 1975/1975, Paris: UGE, 1976.

28   Macciocchi recounts this clash at great length in the postface to vol. 2 of *Eléments*. Natacha Michael published a polemical pamphlet against Macciocchi a couple of years later: *Contre M.A. Macciocchi : contribution à la critique d'une nouvelle branche de la science, la raciologie politique*, Marseille: Ed. Potémkine, 1978. The Groupe foudre was an offshoot of the UCFML, the Maoist group co-founded by Michel, Sylvain Lazarus and Alain Badiou.

29   Maria Antonietta Macciocchi, 'Les femmes et la traversée du fascisme', in *Eléments pour une analyse du fascism*, vol. 1, 128–278; Macciocchi, *La donna 'nera'*; Macciocchi, 'Female Sexuality in Fascist Ideology', *Feminist Review* 1: 1, 1979: 67–82. For a perceptive overview of the debate on women and fascism, which touches on Macciocchi, as well as 1970s feminist anti-fascism in the UK (the Women and Fascism Study Group, Big Flame, Rock Against Sexism), see David Renton, 'Women and Fascism: A Critique', *Socialist History* 20, 2001, 72–83.

30   Macciocchi, *La donna 'nera'*, 19.

31   Macciocchi, 'Female Sexuality in Fascist Ideology', 80.

32   Ibid., 69. As Macciocchi observes: 'fascism comes to the relief of the church guards. It is able to do this because of the submissiveness of women, whose instincts it can channel into a sort of new religious fervor' (68).

33   Ibid., 70. On the nexus between a feminised necrophilia and the sexualised adulation of Mussolini see also Carlo Emilio Gadda, *Eros e Priapo. Versione originale*, eds Paola Italia and Giorgio Pinotti, Milan: Adelphi, 2016, 93, 108, 237.

34   Macciocchi, 'Female Sexuality in Fascist Ideology', 73.

35   Jane Caplan, 'Introduction to Female Sexuality in Fascist Ideology', *Feminist Review* 1.1 (1979), 62. Mussolini and Hitler both followed Gustave Le Bon's crowd-psychology in constantly figuring the mass as 'female' (irrational, hysterical, emotional, desiring subordination, etc.), when they weren't thinking of it as a passive material for the Leader-as-Artist to sculpt.

36   Ibid., 61–2.

37   Ibid., 65.

38   Macciocchi, 'Female Sexuality in Fascist Ideology', 75.

39   Dagmar Herzog, *Sex after Fascism: Memory and Morality in Twentieth-*

Century Germany, Princeton: Princeton University Press, 2005. I am grateful for Quinn Slobodian for directing me to Herzog's work. See also, for a compelling critical overview of the literature on this question, Ishay Landa, 'The Wandering Womb: Fascism and Gender', in *Fascism and the Masses: The Revolt Against the Last Humans, 1848–1945*, London: Routledge, 2018, 320–53.

40   Theweleit, *Male Fantasies, vol. 2*, 7.

41   Ibid., 259.

42   As the blood and soil ideologue and Nazi Minister of Food and Agriculture Richard Walther Darré declared: 'The Nordic race has always found any negation of the body to be foreign. It was only when the immense shadow of an asceticism hostile to beauty arose in the East that it provoked the eclipse of culture in antiquity.' Quoted in Johann Chapoutot, *Greeks, Romans, Germans: How the Nazis Usurped Europe's Classical Past*, Berkeley: University of California Press, 2016, 181.

43   Tim Mason, 'Women in Germany, 1925–1940', in *Nazism, Fascism and the Working Class*, ed. Jane Caplan, Cambridge: Cambridge University Press, 1995, 192.

44   Ibid., 206. One might add that the most chilling image of the sex lives of fascism is not to be looked for in *Ilse, She-Wolf of the SS* and its ilk, but in the private snapshots of serene and contented family life in the officers' quarters of the extermination camps.

45   Macciocchi, 'Female Sexuality in Fascist Ideology', 67.

46   Ibid., 81; Macciocchi, *La donna 'nera'*, 21.

47   Robyn Marasco, 'Reconsidering the Sexual Politics of Fascism', *Historical Materialism* (blog), 25 June 2021.

48   Ibid. This female antifeminism should be linked to the neofascist capture of the implosion of the nuclear family limned by Rosenberg in 'The Daddy Dialectic': 'The family, simply speaking, splinters under the weight of what it has to make up for in the retraction of state resources under austerity. Contemporary neofascism harvests this splintering – this familial decomposition, which, like a collapsing star, emits a chaos of energy as it is vacuumed into oblivion. Note that, here, neofascism isn't about claiming the moral high ground for itself. Rather, it *exults in performing its perversity.*'

49   Lewis and Seresin suggest that there is 'a kind of Eros running through the archive of the far-right wing of women's rights: it appears palpable to us in the pleasures people take in exercising maternalist authoritarianism, in

the euphoria of the womanhood-as-suffering worldview, in the wounded attachment undergirding same-sex cis separatism … There is an excited, sacrificial kind of doom that attends the condition of being so-called women-born women, in the eyes of participants in eugenic feminism.' Sophie Lewis and Asa Seresin, 'Fascist Feminism: A Dialogue', *Transgender Studies Quarterly* 9: 3, 2022, 464, 469–70.

50 As the artist and AIDS activist David Wojnarowicz quipped in the 1980s about the efforts by the US Republican Senator Jesse Helms to block federal funding for any programme mentioning homosexuality: 'Fascists wearing conservative drag have mounted Helms and ridden him through the foundations of the Constitution.' *Close to the Knives: A Memoir of Disintegration*, London: Serpent's Tail, 1992, 129.

51 Natasha Chang, *The Crisis-Woman: Body Politics and the Modern Woman in Fascist Italy*, Toronto: University of Toronto Press, 2015. Discussed in Serena Bassi and Greta LaFleur, 'Introduction: TERFS, Gender-Critical Movements, and Postfascist Feminisms', *TSQ: Transgender Studies Quarterly* 9: 3, 2022, 315.

52 Cara Daggett, 'Petro-masculinity: Fossil Fuels and Authoritarian Desire', *Millennium: Journal of International Studies* 47: 1, 2018, 44. On the psychological wages of fossil authoritarianism, see also Malm and Zetkin Collective, *White Skin, Black Fuel*.

53 Klaus Theweleit, 'Postface', in Littell, *Le sec et l'humide*, 124. Among the institutions mentioned by Theweleit, via Rigoberta Menchù, is the Latin American death squad, which manifests one of the universal features of the corporeal fascism analysed by Theweleit, namely 'an *authorised transgression towards crime*, which exhibits itself at the same time as it is carried out' (124).

54 On queer anti-fascism, see Rosa Hamilton, 'The Very Quintessence of Persecution: Queer Anti-fascism in 1970s Europe', *Radical History Review* 138, 2020, 60–81.

55 Bassi and LaFleur, 'Introduction: TERFS, Gender-Critical Movements, and Postfascist Feminisms', *TSQ: Transgender Studies Quarterly* 9: 3, 318. See also the effort to excavate a capitalist logic of abstraction behind fascist transmisogyny and anti-Semitism, personified in the figure of the Jew as inventor of transgenderism, in Joni Alizah Cohen, 'The Eradication of "Talmudic Abstractions": Anti-Semitism, Transmisogyny and the National Socialist Project', *Verso* blog, 19 December 2018.

56   I am inspired here by Dorian Bell's incisive discussion of 'racial scalarity' in Bell, *Globalizing Race*.

57   Consider, for instance, institutions like the World Congress of Families and the plea for the heteronormative family made by the post-fascist Italian PM Giorgia Meloni at its 2019 meeting in Verona. Meloni is a frequent purveyor of the Great Replacement narrative.

58   See Theweleit, *Male Fantasies, vol. 2*, as well as Rabinbach and Benjamin's foreword to the volume.

59   Theweleit quotes the 'Nazi dream' of one of its chief ideologues, Alfred Rosenberg: 'Some intangible impulse within the masses has long wished to rid itself of the wretched belief that life is intended for pleasure – a contagious belief which is truly Jewish in nature. Today, the idyll of "heaven on earth" has lost much of its attraction.' Theweleit comments: 'This quotation from Rosenberg is a highly explicit formulation of the Nazi program for the masses: a combating of any hope for a real "heaven-on-earth", a real life in pleasure; a naming of the desire for a better life as an illness, of human pleasures as a contagious disease whose prime carrier is the "Jewish element", with its perpetual drive toward miscegenation.' Theweleit, *Male Fantasies, vol. 2*, 9. Fascism: eros without happiness, desire without pleasure? As Alexandra Minna Stern writes, referencing Jason Stanley, for the US far right, 'obliterating the possibility of gender fluidity is integral to the restoration of patriarchal white America'. Stern, *Proud Boys and the White Ethnostate*, 134.

Conclusion

1   Ernst Fraenkel's 1941 *The Dual State* (which posited the co-existence in Nazi Germany of a Normative State for 'Aryan' citizens and a Prerogative State 'beyond the law' for the rest) is one of the frameworks that the late Hungarian philosopher and anti-fascist intellectual G. M. Tamás drew upon to identify 'hostility to universal citizenship' as the thread connecting fascism to post-fascism, for which he also revived Seymour Martin Lipset's formula 'the extremism of the centre'. See G. M. Tamás, 'On post-fascism', *Boston Review*, 1 June 2000.

2   Brendan O'Connor, *Blood Red Lines: How Nativism Fuels the Right*, Chicago: Haymarket, 2021, 127. While centred on the United States, O'Connor's coinage of border fascism and his compelling delineation

of its reliance as an ideology on a whole infrastructure of far-right philanthropy, think tanks, etc. can be usefully transposed to other scenarios.

3   Gilmore, *Abolition Geography*, 451, 495.

4   Ibid., 306.

5   Mike Giglio, 'Mirrorglass: How Jan. 6 Brought Frontier Violence to the Heart of U.S. Power', *The Intercept*, 3 January 2023.

Index